Keepsake Letters

Keepsake Letters

Collections of Love and Remembrance
from 9/11 Family Members

Collected by Tuesday's Children

iUniverse, Inc.
Bloomington

Keepsake Letters
Collections of Love and Remembrance from 9/11 Family Members

iUniverse books may be ordered through booksellers or by contacting:

iUniverse
1663 Liberty Drive
Bloomington, IN 47403
www.iuniverse.com
1-800-Authors (1-800-288-4677)

ISBN: 978-1-4620-3747-6 (sc)
ISBN: 978-1-4620-3748-3 (ebk)

Printed in the United States of America

iUniverse rev. date: 11/02/2011

INTRODUCTION

To Our Families,

On behalf of Tuesday's Children, I am honored to present to you this Keepsake Book, full of loving and inspirational tributes to your family members.

Tuesday's Children's staff and our partner, Brian Curtis, have been overwhelmed by the response to our book project and we send our sincere gratitude for your participation. I know writing these letters may have been emotional or difficult, but the end result is a loving tribute to your loved one.

Much has happened since September 11th, 2001, but we continue to move forward. Tuesday's Children remains committed to providing programs and support for all of you in the years to come.

My deepest appreciation goes to Sara Wingerath and Molly Lieberman for their dedication to this project and to Brian Curtis, for providing his guidance and expertise.

We hope that you will be as inspired by these letters as we are.

Sincerely,
Terry Sears
Executive Director
Tuesday's Children

LARRY JOHN SENKO

Larry John Senko was born on February 20, 1967 in Pittsburgh, Pennsylvania. He grew up in Donora, Pennsylvania with his parents, Ed and Margaret Senko and his older brother, Eddie. He married Debbi Yusem in 1997 and they have a son named Tyler. Larry earned a Bachelor's Degree from St. Francis University and worked as a Vice President for Alliance Consulting. He loved his family and friends, sports, driving fast cars, and playing guitar to the Grateful Dead. On September 11th, Larry was in a meeting in his office on the 102nd floor of the North Tower. He was 34.

Tyler Senko Goldman (Son)
Age: 11

Dear Daddy Larry,

I miss you very much. From when I was a baby to the present, my Mom has always told me terrific things about you. I take after you because I am a great athlete. I play for Pennsbury Travel Baseball. I play outfield and I was an All-Star this year. I had a .360 batting average, .660 on-base and slugging percentage, and a 1.320 OPS in 26 games. I hope you are proud of me.

Thank you for blessing me with a wonderful family, including my sister, Lindsey, my dad, Dan, and my mom, Debbi. I try to be a good big brother. We also have a cat named Callie. The day you died she came to our door so we took her in. Today she is one of my best friends.

I am very smart in school. I am in fifth grade and I am in an advanced math program (AMP). When I grow up I want to be a major league baseball sportscaster, a MLB player, or a forensic scientist.

I try to learn a lot about September 11. I wish you were on a lower floor. I am sorry that happened to you. It must have been scary to know you may not see me again. I love you! I hope to see you in heaven.

Your Son,
Tyler Jay Senko Goldman

MICHAEL C. OPPERMAN

Michael Charles Opperman was born on February 27, 1956 in New York City, New York to Jacob and Anna Opperman. He married Deborah Jongbloed on September 9, 1978 and had two children, Michael Jr. and Elizabeth. Michael loved music, electronics, the New York Mets, his family and his job. He worked for AON on the 103rd floor of Tower 2. He was 45 years old.

Michael Opperman Jr. (Son)
Age: 28

Deborah Opperman (Wife)
Age: 54

Dear Dad,

You were the hardest working person I have ever known. Every weekday, you would get up at 2:30 a.m. to start your commute, getting into the office by 5:00 a.m. Even with such an early start, you wouldn't be home until around seven at night. Then we'd all have dinner, hang out for a bit, and then you would work out, shower, and go to bed by ten. But the most amazing thing was that you never had trouble finding time for us. In fact, I believe it was our family that drove you to work as hard as you did. Boy, were we spoiled. Every second of every day you were either working for us or spending time with us. I honestly don't know how—or even if—you ever found any real time for yourself. I remember you always being there, somehow, even if it seemed impossible to do so. It was as if Clark Kent never missed an appointment but still managed to keep the world safe as Superman. That was you. Whether it was coaching my Little League Baseball team, attending every little academic event I was ever a part of, or simply picking me up from my part-time job 15 minutes early every night so you could buy my dinner. Like I said. Spoiled. Spoiled rotten.

Of course, you never know what you have until it's gone. So true, so true. I was only in my second week of college; a freshman at Wagner College in Staten Island. You called me from work around 8:00 a.m. to remind me that you would stop by later that day with my new printer.

"Sounds good. See you later, Dad," was about all I could muster at such an early hour. That was it. No 'I love you' or 'Thanks for calling.' It was just six simple words, the last four of which would last a lifetime for me. I never did see you later, Dad, because it was September 11th, 2001 and you worked in the World Trade Center.

One of the Wagner College dormitories overlooks the New York skyline. Mine didn't, but my friend's did. She called me moments before I left for class to let me know that there was smoke coming out of the World Trade Center and she asked if everything was all right with you. I turned on the TV to see the horrific scene. I never did go to class that day . . . or that week.

Up until that moment, I never really knew how amazing friends can be. As I became emotionally numb, all of my friends at the school, only one of which I'd known for more than a week, rallied around me, offering to do anything to help me through this. One of them even spent hours on the phone that first night calling around local hospitals to see if you had turned up. It helped so much having such a strong support system. Of course, heading home was still a must.

I tried to process what had just transpired. I was picked up and brought home by Uncle Steve or Uncle Andy or some other relative. I honestly don't remember who it was, which might help paint a picture of how disconnected my body had become. In fact, most of that time was a complete blur. What . . . what just happened? The event was completely incomprehensible.

Once at home, a new thought popped into my head. I was now the man of the house. But I was also an 18 year-old kid starting college with his entire life ahead of him. Fortunately, with Mom's and Beth's blessings and some financial assistance that would help put me through college, I managed to get back to school fairly quickly. My teachers kept telling me to take all the time that I needed and not rush back, but two things kept coming to mind. First, when your world is turned upside down like mine was, you ache for any kind of normalcy you can find. Second, I couldn't let anyone down. Not Mom or Beth, not myself, and especially not you, Dad. I would press on, applying the effort and dedication that you had naturally instilled in me throughout my life. You had been teaching me all the lessons I ever really needed to know about work ethic and family, without me even noticing.

But, at the end of the day, life is really all about learning lessons. If you're lucky, that is. Otherwise, you might miss out on some really great stuff. I know that it is because of you that I work my butt off in everything that I do, no matter how menial the task. And it is because of you that I always think long and hard about what other people need first before worrying about my own needs. As a result, you would be proud to know, Dad, that I'm on my way to finishing my PhD in mathematics. I've been fortunate enough to teach some basic math courses and I loved every minute of it. I hope to become a professor as soon as my degree is finished. Thus, the hard-working part of the equation is slowly coming to fruition. On top of that, I have met the love of my life, Kaitlyn. I wish you could meet her. We are currently planning our wedding for this summer and I couldn't be happier. All I want to do now is to make sure she is happy every second of every day and to one day start a family so that I can pass down the lessons and the legacy that has come to mean so much in my life.

Thanks, Dad. I will always love you.

Michael

Dear Mike,

Of course the most important thing I need to say is how very much I still miss you. I can't even comprehend, how in the world, so much time has passed. And yet my love for you remains so strong. You were my one and only, my own true love and my soul mate.

I am probably frustrating you, but I cannot date. I will not betray what we had. I am not interested in finding someone new. I am still the same girl that you fell in love with. I've always been old fashioned and set in my ways.

We had a great twenty-three years of marriage. We were perfect together. All who knew us as a couple are not surprised that I haven't dated. I don't believe that I will change. I know someday we will be together again. Yes, I have episodes of feeling lonely, but I am trying to offset that by making more friends.

I know you must be proud of me with all that I have accomplished since you are gone. I am just sorry that you never got to enjoy this version of me. I have more interests. I am more social. And I am more assertive. But I think you had to leave in order for me to grow.

You were always my rock and my safe place to fall. We met when I was sixteen. In my late teens I began to suffer from anxiety and panic disorder. It continued throughout our dating years and into our marriage. There were times that it was very challenging for me to leave my home. My anxiety kept me from living a full life. When you passed away, I had lost the one person to whom I had become so dependent upon. I could have just let the anxiety continue to place limits on my existence, but I chose to get better. With the help of a wonderful therapist and hard work on my part, I learned to live with my anxiety disorder. I handled all of the legal and financial matters that needed attending to after 9-11. I was meeting with attorneys, financial advisors and accountants. I also began to make home improvements that we had planned to do. As a single Mom, I raised our daughter through her teenage years. I was getting out there and making friends. Having always been a good listener, I had many people coming to me for support or just to vent their problems and frustrations. I think they saw my strength and felt somehow that if I could do it, they could do it, too. I was no longer living a small life.

I have faced many challenges since you've passed. The hardest was being diagnosed with breast cancer in 2003. I was terrified that our children would lose their only parent. With strength, courage and family support I rallied through my illness. Your untimely death and my cancer diagnosis have given me a greater appreciation of life. It has made me more compassionate, empathetic and less judgmental. I feel that I have found my purpose in life and that is to be an inspiration to others. I have faced much adversity and I have come back, each time, stronger and better than before.

Our children are doing great. Elizabeth just graduated from college. Michael is completing his research for his PhD. in Mathematics. I'm sure that you watch us and see how well they are coping. They miss you, too. All that we do is in honor of you. The entire family loved you so much and miss you dearly.

Please continue to send your signs. I feel your presence often. We are still connected. I appreciate how you still communicate with us. You often come to me in my dreams. Countless times I glance at the clock to see that it's 9:11. I am frequently coming upon numbers that always add up to 11:a parking space number or a number assigned to me at a recent book signing. My indoor chimes strangely ring when I've either mentioned your name or the clock reads 9:11. And the best is that you just seem to know when I need confirmation that you are still with us. I will love and cherish you forever.

Love always,
Debbie

MICHAEL TADDONIO

Michael Taddonio was born in Rockville Center, New York, to Richard and Josephine Taddonio on April 2, 1962. Michael had two brothers, Richard and Marc, and two sisters, Lisa and Terry. Michael grew up in Upper Brookville and attended Locust Valley Schools. He was senior class president. After high school, Michael attended Sienna College in Loudonville, New York, where he majored in business. After graduating Sienna in 1984, Michael became a bond broker. Michael married his wife Denise, on August 20, 1988. Together they had three children, Danielle Rose Taddonio, Nicole Mary Taddonio and Michael Joseph Taddonio. The family resided in Huntington, New York, while Michael worked as a bond broker for Euro Brokers. Michael loved his children and his favorite sports teams, the New York Islanders, Mets and Jets. Michael was 39 years old on September 11, 2001.

Danielle, Nicole and Michael Taddonio (Children)
Ages: 19, 17, 14

Dear Daddy,

We love you so much and we miss you even more.

We try to do the best we can, as you taught us.

We have wonderful memories of you loving us and being the best daddy ever.

Sometimes we just don't understand why you were taken away from us so soon.

It makes us sad that you didn't see us get dressed for the prom or graduate from junior high or high school. They tell us you can see everything we do, and that you are with us all the time. But it just doesn't live up to getting a big daddy hug or seeing that smile on your face.

We each have a piece of you in our hearts every day, no matter what we do or where we go. People tell us we look so much like you and it always makes us feel so proud. Proud that you are our FATHER, our DAD.

We love you Daddy, and we miss you so much.

Love, Danielle, Nicole and Michael

EDMUND MICHAEL McNALLY

Edmund Michael McNally was born on October 6, 1960, in Boston, Massachusetts, to Edmund and Elizabeth McNally, the brother of Lydia, Amy, Katherine (aka Muffin), and Mary. He married Elizabeth McCartney on October 26, 1985, and they have three children, Erin, Brienne and Shannon. Edmund earned a bachelors degree in Biology from Adelphi University, completed a computer science certificate program at Hofstra University and worked for Fiduciary Trust Company International for more than ten years during which time he attained his last position of Senior Vice President—Director of Technology. He was a dedicated and fun loving husband, father and friend. He loved to entertain, cook, golf, garden, but most of all, enjoyed summer days relaxing at the beach with his family and a good cigar. On September 11th, Edmund was on the 97th floor of the South Tower. When the first plane struck the North Tower, he was evacuating coworkers and was coordinating the implementation of the technology disaster recovery plan. He was 40 years old.

Shannon McNally (Daughter)
Age: 18

Dear Dad,

I believe when you experience something catastrophic you become recreated by the experience. I was in the arms of a loved one; your arms that kept me safe. I thought nothing could go wrong, my life was going along and I believed what I had was invincible. I thought everyone had this, everyone in my world at least. Because I was sheltered. But when disaster occurs, who could shelter me then?

I walked into my house, a house full of family on my sister's birthday. There are no smiles, but instead tears, and although I am frozen, my legs don't stop. They continue to walk into the living room. That is when my perfect life as I knew it, ended.

My world broke into pieces.

Days began to go by without someone I thought would never go away.

And now I don't have your arms to keep me safe; instead, I am left with reoccurring thoughts the way everything burned and eventually fell.

I imagine the final calls you made to Mom. I imagine the words that flowed through the line as her tears fell to the floor knowing what the outcome was.

The planes hit and the towers fell. I remember being so proud to tell my friend I had been to the 97th floor where my dad worked, like his second home almost, it was normal, only now normal would never be normal again.

Those buildings are so close to me. They never leave my side. They never leave my thoughts. My normal life became extraordinary in seconds. Now the buildings I was so proud of would make me vulnerable to a world I never really knew. I have seen the world in a different way.

In some ways, I will forever see the world as I saw it that day.

They say that you were an intelligent man who I learned could function in a life or death situation. That day, you knew it was death. You knew what was at the end of the tunnel. The planes had crashed underneath your floor so there was no way out; you knew and told Mom it was a terrorist attack. You felt the explosions underneath you.

The floor was hot and it was hard to breathe. But you never failed to keep your priorities in order. You told Mom everything she had to do in detail.

I believe everything in this world is connected in some way and that everything comes together through death. I believe my experience has recreated me and reshaped who I was into who I am. I am proud of my scars of my experience I will not hide them but illuminate them; I will use my experience to remind myself what I have overcome.

I believe when you experience something catastrophic, you become recreated by your experience.

Love,
Shannon

WALWYN STUART

Walwyn W. Stuart Jr. was born in Brooklyn, New York to Doris and Walwyn Stuart, Sr. on February 13, 1973. He was the youngest of seven children including Adolph, Diedra, Edwyn, Olga, Keisha, and Monette. He married Thelma Lewis in 1997 and has a daughter Amanda who was born on September 28, 2000. Walwyn graduated from Westinghouse High in Brooklyn, New York. He studied for two years at SUNY Stony Brook prior to being called to NYPD in 1993 to pursue his dream of becoming a police officer. He was a Detective Investigator with the Manhattan North Narcotics Division and the Organized Crime Control Bureau in the Narcotics Division until accepting his assignment in the PATH Division with the Port Authority Police Department in 2000. He was affectionately called "Sweetie" by his wife, "Stuwey" by his colleagues, and "Wiz" by some friends. He had a relentless desire to excel, and an impeccable moral character. Walwyn loved playing chess, performing magical tricks, sports, serving in several ministries at the Brooklyn Tabernacle Church and was loyal to family, friends and colleagues alike. His Christian faith was vital to his life. He was 28 years of age when he died at the World Trade Center, possibly in Tower Two on September 11th, 2001, while serving in an official capacity.

Amanda Stuart (Daughter)
Age: 10

Dear Daddy,

I hope I'll meet you one day face to face. Everyone keeps telling me what a great man you were. Just know I love you and care about you. I am always thinking about you through the tough times and the good times. I wish you were here with me and Mommy. I know you are in an amazing place right now. No matter what happens, you will always be my big Hero.

Love always,
Your daughter, Amanda Stuart

RANDY SCOTT

Randy Scott was born May 27, 1953 in Brooklyn, New York to Lillian Scott; he was the youngest of the five siblings; Bonnie-Ann, Jacquie, Georgia and Deborah. He was the baby brother, the only male, and the apple of his mother's eye. Randy married Denise Castiglioni in November 1979 and they have three daughters, Rebecca, Jessica and Alexandra. After studying at Brooklyn Tech, he went to work as an International Money Market Manager, Broker/Dealer. He enjoyed vacationing in Hilton Head Island, South Carolina, with his family and spending time on his beloved couch. On the morning of September 11th, Randy was at his desk at Euro Brokers Inc. on the 84th floor of the North Tower. He was 48 years old.

Debbie Scott-Arena (Sister)
Age: 60

Dear Randy,

It's true what they say; everything comes in threes. We lost our mom, our sister, and then you. It was a dreadful day, one that I will never forget and one that affects us every day. There is a constant reminder—in the news, in books, in passing conversation, every time we drive over the George Washington Bridge—of how we lost you and a part of ourselves. It will never be the same and accepting this has been the hardest for all of us.

The kids miss your jokes, your sense of humor, and your determination. Joey looked up to you so much and admired everything about the man you are. I can't believe that it has been almost ten years. It's hard to understand why this happened. It doesn't make any sense. But thinking of you and all of our memories makes me smile. I know my children think of the family vacations and "bother Uncle Randy" and it's comforting to know that each moment was enjoyed. I only wish there could have been time to create more memories.

We are all doing as best we can and we are moving on at our individual paces. I know you would be proud of all of us. You would be ecstatic to see your three daughters all grown up. And rest assured that whenever the girls need us, we are there for them. Your wife Denise misses you in every way possible. She misses the simplicity of her days, those evening walks around the block, cooking an early dinner and you taking the time to help set up her classroom. She misses her husband.

You had such a yearning and zest for life. It was contagious. You loved, you did, you supported and you gave to all, especially those less fortunate. I miss the power and energy behind you. I miss your laughter, I miss you asking . . . "Where's my hug?" Everyone wanted a piece of you. To this day, I believe you have given your family, your friends and your acquaintances just that. Your sincerity, your thoughtfulness, your concern for others, will be remembered by all. You touched so many lives and everyone is a better person for having known you.

Thinking of you now, I can breathe better, think clearer. At times, struggling myself, I realize even though you are not here with me, I will always be surrounded by your thoughts and energy. You are never far from my heart.

If there is one thing I could ask you . . . . why did you go to work that day? You should have played golf. I miss you.

Love as always,
Your favorite sister, (LOL)
Debbie

BRIAN MURPHY

Brian Joseph Murphy was born on March 21st, 1960, in Westfield, Massachusetts, to Harold and Tina Murphy. His siblings include Ann, Harold, and Cindy Murphy. He married Judy Bram in 1994 and they had two children, Jessica and Leila. Brian earned a BA from Williams College and an MBA from Columbia University. He worked for Cantor Fitzgerald. He loved his wife, two daughters, and many friends, and he enjoyed sports, cooking, and reading. On September 11th, Brian was at his desk on the 106th floor of the World Trade Center. He was 41 years old.

Jessica Murphy (Daughter)
Age: 15

Dear Dad,

I was just five years old when you were taken from us. I woke up that morning and went to school. It was a perfectly sunny, normal day in early September. Nobody had any idea what was to happen that day. I was just a little kid in kindergarten, and I definitely did not know that I would never see you again.

"Alright, everyone, let's just get to the other classroom so the entire grade can be together in a remotely organized fashion."

"Okay, children. It's all right. Just a little accident."

These falsehoods were spoken by Mrs. Simon, my teacher, as we shuffled next door. Her so-called "soothing" words temporarily quieted the inquiries of some of the children in our class, but I was even more confused when my uncle picked me up from school a little bit later. You and Mom switched off picking me up: one would get Leila at nursery school and one would pick me up. On this particular September day, it was your turn. It was a little unsettling when Uncle Steven showed up, but there was much more distress to come.

When I got home, there were already several relatives in our apartment. Then Mom, Leila and Grandma all came together. I knew something was wrong, but I wasn't entirely sure what. Mom, in particular, seemed like she was ready to faint. Later in the day, I found out what had happened to you. At first, it was just a trance-like nightmare. Pretty soon it was very realistic. Mom was a single parent.

You were a tall, broad-shouldered man. Six-foot two, but in person, you didn't really seem that big. You made me feel safe and comfortable. You weren't big to me. Actually, everybody loved you. You were kind, funny, and pleasant to be around. And you were so loyal. Mom told me a story about a call you received at 2:30 a.m. one night.

"Hey, Brian, I'm really sorry to be bothering you at this hour, but I really need your help," gasped John, one of your many friends. John was close to tears. His car had broken down in a bad neighborhood, and he wanted some advice.

"No problem, I'll be there in a second."

Mom told me that you got out of bed, drove to John and waited with him until his car got towed. Then, you drove John back home. You did anything to help anyone, simply out of empathy and compassion.

Not only did you mean well, but you knew a lot as well. A few years after you died, Mom, Leila and I were interviewed by the alumni magazine of Brown University, Mom's alma mater.

"Most people either know a little bit about a lot of different things or a lot about one specific topic, but Brian knew a lot about everything," Mom told the reporter. It was true. You could fix household appliances, you could name all of the plants we passed on a hike through the woods and, from what Mom tells me, you were a great businessman.

But above everything else, you were a great father. I have very few memories of you, Dad, but I have one recollection of when you came home at the end of the day and said, "How are my three little girls?"

Dad, unfortunately, Leila and I never really got to know you. Much of what we know and remember we learned from Mom and family and friends. But I do know this: I love you more than ever and I know you are watching over us.

Love,
Jessica

BRENDA CONWAY

Brenda E. Conway was born February 19, 1961 in New York City to Edith and William Alexander. She had two sisters, Linda and April and one brother, Stanley. Brenda married Russell K. Conway in 1985, and they had two children, Danielle and Mandell. Brenda attended Lehman College and Monroe College before embarking on her career. Brenda loved to read, shop and motivate youth. On September 11, 2001, she worked for Marsh and McLennan, Tower 1, 97th floor. She was 40 years old.

Edith Watford (Mother)
Age:72

Dear Brenda,

September 11, 2001 was the day that my life changed forever. We spent the Sunday of September 9, 2001 together at church, laughing and rejoicing, on what would be our last time together.

The tragedy affected my mind so much that I can't recall the last words I said to you. I do remember you by the love and support that you gave me as a mom and to the ministry. You were a true, dedicated Christian and a loving and caring person.

I do find peace and joy in knowing that we will be together throughout eternity.

Love,
Mom

STEVEN POLLICINO

Steve Pollicino was born on February 2, 1953, in Brooklyn, New York. He grew up in Hicksville, attending Nassau Community College where he met Jane Elefante. After earning a B.S. degree from Long Island University at C.W. Post, Steve spent some years managing his own business. He then joined the Cantor Fitzgerald team and worked as a corporate bond broker, spending fifteen years in the world of finance. Steve and Jane married on April 1st,1978 and had two children, Steven and Celeste. Steve lived each day to its fullest, making life fun and just a little bit happier for everyone who knew him. His greatest pleasure was spending time with his family and friends. He was 48 years old.

Vicki Tureski (Sister-in-Law)
Age: 57

Dear Steve,

I miss you. I miss you. I miss you. I say it every day. I can say it a thousand times and it never changes. It doesn't go away. The miss is always the same size, the same shape, the same feeling. It still hurts physically in my stomach to think about your absence. I can't think for too long about the fact that you are no longer here on this earth because I will go out of my mind. I can't go there. I put it away. Even after all this time I just can't face the fact that you are gone. Where are you?

Sometimes I play the game where I think you're still at work. Not healthy, I know, but it's a safe place to put "it." And if you were still at work, wouldn't you be calling the house asking, "Hey Vic. What's up? How are things out there in the Hamptons? What are we doing this weekend? Let's meet for dinner somewhere. I'll call Laraine and Phil." You were always the one to rally everyone together to meet at a restaurant, always insisting on a round table so we could all interact and enjoy each other's company. Your purpose in life was to make sure everyone around you was happy and having a good time. That's what brought you happiness, making sure that everyone else was happy.

I find peace in knowing that you loved your job at Cantor Fitzgerald. You survived the attack in February '93. It took you hours to walk down those stairs while thinking you were not going to get out alive. That experience did not keep you from returning to your job. You felt secure in the measures taken to keep the buildings safe. *"The only way they are going to get this building is by flying a plane into it,"* were your exact words. Oh, how I wish we had stopped you from returning to the 105th floor of the North Tower but why would we? You felt safe and happy. *"I'm on top of the world,"* you would often say. I would often think of you during the day, up there, in the sky, among the clouds. It always made me smile. What a twist of fate that

Collected by Tuesday's Children

"On Top of the World" is the title of Tom Barbash's book about Cantor Fitzgerald, Howard Lutnick, and September 11th.

How lucky were Jane and I to meet you at Nassau Community College. We were all only seventeen years old. You know I pushed Jane to go out with you when we saw you walk in our Biology lab. You learned quickly how Jane and I were a package deal. That's how it is when you are an identical twin. I was so happy when you guys finally got married because it meant that you were officially a part of our family. Not only would we be friends, but you were now officially my brother. April 1st, 1978, was such a happy day.

How perfect were our lives? We were leading ordinary but very perfect lives. Luckily for our family you were just not the typical holiday relative. It was quite the opposite. You were there not only for your own children but you were present for events that mattered to your nieces and nephews as well. You clapped the loudest at their plays, concerts, ballets, hockey games and parades. You were there yelling and cheering. It didn't matter which child was *performing*. You carried on like it was the most important thing happening in the world. I thank you for that show of love and support. I thank you for being such a big part of every little thing that happened in all of our lives.

You promoted cousin sleepovers that including all the cousins; Nicole, Eric, Michelle and Philip. They would join your children, Steven and Celeste, for a night of fun that sometimes included getting OUT of pajamas to go bowling late at night when sleeping should have been taking place. They all counted on you the next morning as well to get the Dunkin' Donuts and bagels. No one else could flatten a bagel the way you did.

"Flatten mine more Uncle Steve. It's not flat enough yet, Uncle Steve. No, it needs to be flatter. Pound harder please."

The hammering could be heard throughout the house as you tried with all your might to "please the kids." The morning that you decided to take a different approach to the bagel preparation is one that all of the kids will remember forever. Determined to get the bagel as flat as possible, you took the cream cheesed bagel and put it in a brown bag. Grabbing the keys to your jeep you walked into the garage. Do you remember how the kids just followed you down there not quite sure what you were about to do? Your sense of suspense and mischief got cooking early in the morning. You placed the bag under the tire of the jeep. You got in the driver's seat and started up the engines! The kids screamed as you rolled the vehicle out of the garage right over the brown bag. They got hysterical again as you put it in reverse and backed over the bagel a second time.

"Is that flat enough for you?" you asked over the laughing that came from those kids.

Thanks for making them always giggle and laugh. Thanks for teaching them how important it is to take the time to do silly things. "Always remember to keep giggling," are the words you said to Celeste and her friend when you picked Celeste up to go home on the evening of September 10, 2001. Were your words a coincidence? I don't think so.

A few days into this tragedy, Steve, we were told to be prepared for "surprises" as we found our way through the days, weeks, and months ahead. A volunteer counselor at one of the first Cantor gatherings was there "to help." She did a lot of talking and there were a few phrases that caught on to us. "Be prepared for surprises," she warned. We thought it was an odd thing for her to say and we dismissed it. Over the past ten years her words did ring true over and over again.

One very early surprise came in the form of a letter. Can you believe we heard from your third grade teacher who wrote all about what a great guy you were even at age eight? Even then you always wore a smile and made others happy. She even spoke of your eyebrows. I will just leave that alone for now. Another "surprise" story that found its way to us is what you really did with all of those cans and bottles that were bagged by Jane for their return to the store for refund. We found out, Steve, that all those years, not one of those bags made it to the store. Actually it didn't surprise us to learn that you had befriended a homeless man at the Hicksville train station. Giving him the bag of returns became your routine. We were gifted with many of these stories about your acts of kindness following September 11th. They were, in fact, lovely surprises.

So again, I say, I miss you Steve. I miss everything about you. I miss the way you would steal the meatballs out of the pot on macaroni Sundays at my parents' house. I am grateful that you would always show up and shovel their walk whenever it snowed. I miss the way you managed to take care of all of us on so many levels, in so many ways. Thanks for your generous spirit that always worked towards making things right for everyone. I know you took pleasure in that. I witnessed how you lived each day to its fullest. I am proud to call you my brother-in-law. I honor your memory daily by taking into consideration how you would have acted if you were here. I often ask myself, "What would Steve have done?" or "What would Steve have said if he were in this situation?" Walking your talk is the best way of keeping you alive. It is not an easy thing to do.

Jane and I keep your memory alive yearly as we award scholarships to graduating high school seniors. We look forward to speaking about you to the auditoriums that are filled with students about to "enter the world." This is the perfect opportunity to speak about the importance of random acts of kindness. Our Michelle has recently honored your memory by running a triathlon in your name. On September 12th this year, it was so uplifting to be a part of this positive event. She proudly swam, rode and ran 25 miles. She is sure she achieved this accomplishment with "your helping hands." This, too, will become a yearly event. We are learning the importance of balancing our sadness and tears with laughter and joy. How lucky are we to finally have something so important to look forward the day after September 11th.

Steve, I know that the peace in your soul and fire in your heart touched many. We know that whenever the song, "Shout" is heard, that you are not far away. You were the life of the party. Your friends and family still can't understand why you had to leave the party so early to go home. Although a piece of us still waits for you to come walking through the door we know in our hearts that you truly are home. Steve, to be present in the world without you, that's the hardest thing. But being present in this world is the only way to find you again. We feel you all around us. Keep sending us those signs. Know that you are always in our hearts. Until we meet again my friend. Love you forever.

Always,
Vicki

JEFFREY SHAW

Jeffrey Shaw was born on July 2, 1959 in New York, New York to Charles and Geraldine Shaw, brother of John, Charles, Geraldine, Brian and Richard. He married Debbie Crosby in 1983 and they have two children, Michael and Nicole. Jeff went on to DeVry College before starting his career as an Electrician for Local 3 I.B.E.W for 21 years. He loved his wife, children and family, the St. Louis Rams, hunting and golfing. On September 11, 2001, when Jeff last spoke to Debbie, he was on the 105th floor running a job for Cantor Fitzgerald. Most of his career was spent working in the North Tower (1) for Cantor. Jeff was 42 years old.

Debbie Shaw (Wife)
Age: 40

Steven Choolfaian (Friend)
Age: 51

Hi Babe,

I really don't know where to start, since I tell you everything that goes on as it happens. I do want you to know that not a day goes by that we don't think about you or that your name doesn't come up in the house.

Speaking of the house, it's really starting to get lonely around here, but I know you are as happy and proud as I am of your two children. Jeff, they turned out to be two amazing adults with all the qualities that we as parents strived to instill in them.

Michael graduated Molloy College in 2007, tried the electrician thing like his dad for awhile but it just wasn't for him. While he was in college, he coached basketball at Kellenberg High School and loved it. He is now 25 years-old and a police officer in Manhattan and dating a very nice girl, Christina. He is so much like you. Where you would put your pants under your mattress and nap while the wrinkles came out, he just throws them in the dryer over and over and naps. He is strong yet quiet, very funny and so easy going. He has absolutely become the best person he could be. Unfortunately, he takes after Pops not you when it comes to being handy—he's not at all! Thank God for Uncle Jim.

Nikki (Daddy's little girl) is now 21, and she has a lot of me and your sister's attitude, so say no more. But she is you in so many ways. From the stubbornness to the chocolate she has to have after dinner; from being able to fix things around here to working the computer, she learned so much from you in a short time. Thank goodness someone listened to you when you were always trying to get us to learn that computer. Remember that talk you had with her in August of 2001 about school, since she hated it so much? Well, she never forgot that promise she made to you, and she is now in her senior year in college, majoring in Sign Language. And—get this—she is now in Maryland going to school. Can you believe that she actually went away? She wants to teach the hearing impaired sign language and be an interpreter. Jeff, she is amazing at it and it is so touching to see her communicate with her deaf friends. She is such a strong and beautiful person inside and out. We could not be any more proud of her.

Then there's me. Well, I'm still doing my thing, working at the Island Garden with Jim and Roe. Thanks to so many great friends who helped me get through all those dark days, and who are still there for me now, I am doing O.K. I know that you would want me to move on and be happy, Babe, but first I had the excuse that I had to raise our kids. Now that they are grown, I guess the truth is, I'm just not ready. Maybe when I don't hear your voice like it was yesterday, saying that "it doesn't look good, Babe, and remember I'll always love you" or maybe when I walk into a room and someone makes me feel like I'm the most important person there like you did, I'll know it's right. Until then, you have my heart and you always will. You were my soulmate, and no one can every take your place.

Love you,
Always & Forever
Debbie

Dear Jeff,

We met in the summer of 1969 in Wurtsboro Hills, New York when you were just a year older than my nine. We immediately became what I thought would be lifelong friends; that is, until the terrorists struck us on 9/11/01.

Remember when we grew up that you would ask your Mom if I could stay for the week while my Mom went to work? She would always convince my father to allow me but, of course, our house was off limits. We went in anyway, and we tried to cover our tracks and keep the house as neat as possible. We all decided to sleep at my house—you know, so we could smoke and be adult-free. One morning, you awoke and went to the bathroom. I assumed that you were not going back to bed, so I made the bed as if no one was sleeping in it. When you returned, you saw that the bed was made and you bellowed, "Oh boy, Steven I just got up to use the bathroom." It is a phrase I still do not live down to this date.

You are truly in my thoughts every day of my life and you are greatly missed.

Love,
Steve

STEVEN SCHLAG

Steven Francis Schlag was born on April 17, 1960 in the Bronx, New York, to Patricia A. and Donald J. Schlag. He has two sisters, Jean Marie Nebbia and Ellen Anne Hughes. Steven married Tomoko Tsurko in 1989 and has three children, Dakota, Garrett and Sierra. He earned a B.A. in finance from Montclair State College and worked for Cantor Fitzgerald. He loved his family and always took them skiing, camping, hiking and cycling. On September 11, 2001, Steven was on the 105th floor of the North Tower of the World Trade Center. He was 41 years old.

Patricia A. Schlag (mother)
Age: 75

Hi Steven,

This is Mom. I can still feel you as you moved around inside of me and no one in the whole world can ever understand this . . . so this is our secret. I hope that you are in a better place than we are . . . you are so missed by so many and maybe someday we will all go home and be together . . . there is so much I can say but time is limited . . . there is no way to say an ending to this except,

I'll see you soon.

MOM

FAUSTINO APOSTOL, JR.

Faustino Apostol, Jr. was born on April 15, 1946 in Manhattan, New York to Lina and Fausto Apostol. He is the brother of Theresa Camp and Margaret Apostol. He married his high school sweetheart, Kathleen Neville in 1968. They have two sons, Justin and Christopher, two daughters-in-law, Debi and Jen and six grandchildren: Michael, Alexa, Riley, Katherine, Griffin and Kerrick. Faust was a NYC Firefighter for Engine 55, Battalion 2 in Little Italy for 28 years and loved every minute of it. Faust loved being a grandfather and became known as "PaPa Faust". He was a hard-working man who enjoyed spending time with his family and friends, vacationing, music and cars—he loved life! On September 11, 2001, Faust and his FDNY Battalion 2 brothers arrived on the scene of the World Trade Center's North Tower. He was 55 years old.

Debi Apostol (Daughter-in-Law)
Age: 42

Dear PaPa Faust,

Oh, how we missed you today. It was Michael's opening day of fall baseball, and it was a beautiful day, but you were not there. It is a constant void. There have been so many wonderful moments in our lives the past ten years that we really miss sharing with you.

You have quite a few more grandchildren—four to be exact. We know how happy and BUSY you would have been, and OH, SO PROUD!!! We often think about all the pictures you would be showing of the grandchildren to your friends and co-workers at Engine 55 or SIUH.

Michael is now 10 and so very smart. He absolutely loves baseball and the Yankees. He has been on the All-Star team for three years now and Kathy has enjoyed watching him every moment. We also have our little Alexa, who is now six. She is an absolute joy. I am sure when Kathy talks to you about her, she is sure to tell you how funny she is and so beautiful. Not a day goes by that we don't wish you could see them (though we know you can). Kathy has been busy with all the grandchildren, two in New Jersey and four in Long Island, and she says she can never move from your house because she is right in the middle of all of us. We know she misses you greatly. Losing you on September 11th 2001 was a tremendous loss for all of us. You were everyone's guide. You always had so much to offer us. It is one of many things we miss not having you here anymore. We often think about how much the kids could have learned from you. Even though we see many of your fine, funny and curiousness (being kind here) traits in Michael.

Nine years, ten years, twenty years, it really doesn't matter. The sadness is still the same. The loss is still felt the same way it was on September 12, 2001. We go on; we celebrate many things. Actually, we celebrate almost anything we possibly can but with you always in our hearts and minds. We do have so many things we are thankful and grateful for. We have a wonderful family, our two beautiful children, our home (which you know I loved from Day One and now I love even more). It has become that palatial hide-a-way you loved so much, and you would be so proud. We have great, great friends on our block and, of course, all those wonderful memories of you.

Thank you for always giving us so much of yourself. The memories we have are priceless. We miss you greatly and think of you always. Please continue to watch over all of us, especially the grandchildren.

WE LOVE YOU!!!

Kathy, Debi, Justin, Michael and Alexa

MARK LAWRENCE CHARETTE

Mark Lawrence Charette was a Senior Vice-President at Marsh and McLennan; a former Lieutenant in the US Navy; a loving husband; devoted father, caring son and brother and a remarkable man of strength and integrity. Mark was born on February 19, 1963 in Warwick, Rhode Island, to Lawrence and Donnalee Charette, brother to Gregory. He graduated with a Bachelor of Science degree from the University of Pennsylvania's Wharton School. There, he met his wife, Cheryl Desmarais. They had three children: Lauren, Andrew and Jonathan. They were 8, 6 and 1 on September 11, 2001. Mark was an incredible father who somehow managed to spend an enormous amount of time with his family. He loved wood working, golfing and skiing, hiking and camping with his family. Although Mark's office was in New Jersey, on September 11th, he was holding annual planning meetings for his group at the Marsh offices on the 100th floor of the North Tower. Mark was 38 years old.

Andrew Charette (Son)
Age: 16

Jonathan Charette (Son)
Age: 11

Cheryl Desmarais (Wife)
Age: 48

Dear Dad,

I miss you very much. In the hope that others may know more about you and the great father that you were, I will tell them my greatest memory of how you helped me.

You were always around, despite the fact you worked for Marsh and McLennan, you were always available to play with all three of us. I remember waiting for your return from work, either because I had finished a day of kindergarten or because I was not yet in school. During that particular day, I had gotten into my mind the crazy idea that I would build a bow and arrow. Being four or five, having spontaneously decided to build a bow and arrow, I was at the age that when I wanted something, it was all I could think about. And it was in this state of mind when you came home and found me. Before you had walked five steps into the house, I asked you if you could build a bow and arrow with me. I believe I told you of my several failed attempts earlier. Being who you were, living first for your wife and children, your immediate reply was "of course". And within twenty minutes of getting home from work, you were in the backyard helping me pick out the wood for a bow.

Like the rest of my life, in building this bow and arrow, you were always teaching me things. In this particular case, it was that we must select a wood that is not dead and that can bend; or, when you draw back the bow, the wood will shatter, something I had learned from previous attempts. The second thing that I learned that day was that you do not carve the wood into a bow shape. Rather, you bend it into that shape when you string it so that it retains tension. While adding to the wealth of other random knowledge I have gathered, the real lesson that I learned in building this bow was that you would do anything for me, always. It was lessons like this that you were teaching me.

"There's a right way and an easy way" you would often say, in the hope of teaching us good morals.

That's your story, my favorite memory. I hope it was one of your favorites too.

I miss you,
Andrew

Dear Dad,

Hey, Dad, this letter is my tribute to you. I can still remember when you would have to go to the Home Depot and I would hold up my arms and say "Up" and you would pick me up and take me with you. I also remember when we sat at the table one night and I was sitting in my high chair next to you as we ate mash potatoes. I flung a spoonful across the room and it landed on the floor. You laughed. I loved that moment. I miss you, Dad.

I think you would be so proud of me and all that I have done. I'm playing tennis and doing gymnastics and a lot of other things like that. I'm really good at baseball and I'm taking acting classes at the Paper Mill Playhouse and in the City. I've been running cross country and I am training for a half-marathon. And a few months ago, I went fishing with Pepe and I got my first bee sting. And we are now friends with my kindergarten teacher's family and she actually was the person who you met with and talked about Lauren when you were looking at the Darcy School.

Dad, I have some questions I never got to ask you.

Did you play any other sports other than volleyball? Did you ever fish with Pepe?

I love you and miss you so much.

With love and heart,
Jonathan

Dear Mark,

As I write this letter, it's been nine years since I last saw you. Sometimes it feels like an eternity and sometimes it feels like just yesterday; I remember it so clearly. I remember how you kissed me goodbye and told me you wouldn't be home late. I remember waiting and waiting for you to call not really considering you could be gone. I was convinced you would get out of the building; you had proved to me and the kids time and again there was nothing you couldn't do. I think that's why we had such a difficult time accepting what had happened to you. I remember not knowing where your meeting was, which tower or on what floor. Later that afternoon, when I found out that you were on the 100th floor of the North Tower, I began to get concerned because I knew if you were above where the plane hit, you would never walk by a single person on your way out of the building that needed help.

People say that absence makes the heart grow fonder, but you know that when you were alive the kids and I thought you were perfect: the perfect father; the perfect husband; the perfect partner.

They say it gets better with time, and I guess I have to admit it is better—but not really. I think about you every day and I still miss you so much my heart hurts. I try and remember you and the time we had together, without thinking too much about what it would be like if you were still here because that's just too painful, especially when I think of what a difference it would have made in the life of our kids. I never thought I would be raising them be myself, but I am. They've grown so much and you would be so proud of them. In 2001, Lauren was only eight, just starting third grade and only a green belt in karate. Now she's driving, looking at colleges and holds a second-degree black belt. She is confident and creative. Andrew was just starting first grade but already reading and showing signs that he would do well in school. Now at fifteen, he's the man of the house, earning straight A's and focusing on getting into our alma mater—Wharton. He's charming and responsible. Jon was only one when we lost you, just a baby and not even talking yet. Now, at ten, he has a lot to say about everything. The only one with blonde hair and blue eyes, he's the spitting image of you and has your beautiful singing voice. He is talented and free spirited.

Nothing is more important to me than raising the children the way we would have if you were still here. I try so hard to instill your values in them—your honesty and your integrity, first and foremost. I may not be doing it the way you would have, and for that I am truly sorry. I remember how often you said, "There is the right way and the easy way." You always choose the right way. I also remember how many times you said to the kids, "You can pay me now or pay me later". I'm trying to get them to be the type of people who make the right choices, like you did; but as you know, I was always the 'pay me later' type.

I've tried to maintain many of our family traditions. We still go every year to cut down our own Christmas tree and the children still hang their stockings and I read them *The Night before Christmas* the way you used to. After 9/11, I tried to keep their bedtime routine the same; reading to them, singing to them and rocking them to sleep every night. When I tried to sing to them, it wasn't the same. Though he was only one when you died, Jonathan knew enough, that when you sang to him he cuddled closer and fell asleep; when I sang to him, he reached up with his little hand and covered my mouth. I like to think it was because he knew how much it made me miss you. But then again, we've both heard me sing.

Mark, mostly I remember how great you were with the kids. It amazed me how much you could get done while you were watching them and yet still made them feel like they were the center of your attention. You worked full time, traveled on business, and were restoring our 130 year-old Victorian, doing all the carpentry, electrical and plumbing yourself. But you still managed to spend an enormous amount of time with me and the kids. You made us each feel like we were your number one priority. I think that's what I miss most of all.

I remember anytime you said you were going to Home Depot (which was probably three times a week) one, if not all, three of the kids would want to go with you. You never turned them down no matter how much of a hurry you were in. It was incredible how effortless it was for you to gather them up and take them with you. Everything seemed so easy for you. If I said let's go for a bike ride, before I could get the kids ready, four bikes (yours with Jonathan's child seat) were on the roof of the Expedition waiting for the adventure. I remember you wanting me to get some rest when Jonathan was just a baby so you packed up all three kids and took them camping for the weekend by yourself. You even took them to work with you sometimes. Remember how your coworkers laughed and asked if there was a lightning storm in your office because you let them flick the lights on and off while you were working?

When you worked on the house or in the yard the children were always at your side. I remember you mowing the lawn, with Andrew following you around with his toy lawn mower. All the while, Lauren and Jonathan were playing on the swing set you designed and built for them. For months after 9/11, anytime Jonathan heard a power tool, he would ask, "Dada"? Of course, all the things you built with those power tools weren't just part of restoring the house. I remember you making Lauren's doll house table, Andrew's train table and Jonathan's little kitchen table and, of course, the three most amazing pyramids ever seen at an elementary school science fair.

But it certainly wasn't all work. You were so young to have figured out that we had to save and plan for the future but that we also had to enjoy the day. I am so grateful we were able to vacation as much as we did. It provided us so many happy memories. I remember camping at Myrtle Beach, you playing in the water, teaching Lauren and Andrew how to ride the waves. You were the king of building sand castles and camp fires for roasting marshmallows. I remember taking the kids to Vermont in the summer for hiking and biking and in the winter for skiing. I still don't know how you managed to carry four pairs of skis and Jonathan while I just carried the poles and made sure Lauren and Andrew kept up.

Mark, as I write this, it occurs to me that was how our whole life was: you carried most of the weight; you never complained and you made it look easy. You were so strong and so confident. You inspired the children to believe they could do anything and you made me feel safe. I knew we could face anything; everything would be OK as long as we were together. I miss that and I miss you every day.

Forever yours,
Cheryl

JOSEPH HOLLAND

Joseph Holland was born on November 15, 1968 in Bronx, New York, to Carol and Joseph Holland. His siblings included Tara, Mary Jo, Jeanne, Kerry, James, Michele and Brian. He married Kathleen Mahoney in 1997 and they have a son, Joseph, born on September 1, 2001. Joseph Sr. went to Manhattan College and received a Bachelor of Science (Business Administration) Degree. He was the Vice President/ Broker, trading in crude oil and natural gas at Carr Futures, Inc. Joseph loved his family and the New York Yankees and Dallas Cowboys. On September 11th, Joseph was attending a meeting on the 92nd floor in Tower One. He was 32 years old.

Kathy Holland (Wife)
Age: 42

Joe Holland Jr. (Son)
Age: 10

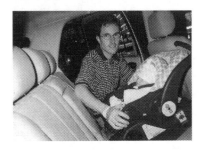

Tara Holland (Sister)
Age: 36

Carol Holland O'Toole (Mother)
Age: 65

Ellen Mahoney (Mother-in-Law)
Age: 68

Dear Joe,

I was sitting here looking at our son, Joe, who looks so much like you, and wondering why things happen? Is there a plan or do things happen merely by chance? It was, I think, by plan and not chance, that you and I met in January 1993. It was just a watering hole on the Upper Eastside that we frequented over the years. I remember how you tried time and time again to teach me how to play pool, something I never quite got the hang of despite you being such a great teacher.

Our love continued to grow. I remember all the fabulous vacations we took together, one more beautiful than the next. All the fun that we had playing golf and drinking pina coladas on the beach. It was on one of those trips that you proposed to me making me the happiest woman alive.

You know one of the things that I loved about you was your sense of humor. Your humor touched those who knew you. I recall how many times you would make me laugh when I needed to. You loved everything about me, especially the sound of my laugh. Now, little Joe loves to see me laugh. What is truly remarkable today is that I see your same humor in our son.

One thing that you were very serious about was being a dad. You took all the prenatal and childcare classes with me and even were my coach for the delivery. The joy when our son was born on September 1 was overwhelming. I know that all you wanted was to be a dad and spend time with our newborn son.

Often I think, what if you had stayed home on 9/11? You did not work at the WTC and had been staying home with me since I had just given birth. However, by chance or by plan, a meeting was called for that morning at the WTC. You attended, bringing your cigars and baby pictures, kissing me goodbye and telling me how much you loved me.

Joe was just 10 days old. He never got to do all those things with you that we dreamed about. You would have loved him so much. Every time I look at him I see you. He is a truly wonderful son, full of love, laughter and kindness. A son, not by chance, but according to plan, so much like his Dad. You would have been so proud.

Joe, you are always in our hearts and memories.

Love always,
Kathy

Dear Dad,

I miss you.

Mom told me that you were very funny. People think I am funny, too. I tell jokes and people laugh. I have lots of friends and I know you did, too.

Everyone says that I remind them of you. I wish I could see you.

I play baseball. I catch, pitch and play first base. I was on the all-star team. I love to watch all sports. My favorite baseball team is the New York Yankees. I know that the Yankees were your favorite team also. Mom has the New York Yankee hat that you brought for me when I was a baby.

I love you,
Joe

Dear Joe,

Believe it or not, even though it's almost ten years later, I still can't truly believe you're gone. It just doesn't seem fair. I never thought I'd have to live my life without my big brother. For as long as I can remember, you were always there for me, guiding me in your big brother way to do the right thing.

Oh, how I miss you! There's been so many times when you're the first person I want to call and tell about something that just happened—and then I remember that I can't. So instead, I imagine what you would say and it brings a smile to my face every single time!

I hold on to our childhood memories as hard as I can so I can keep a piece of you with me. And every time I need you, I find you there in those memories. I laugh out loud sometimes thinking about some of them . . . like our walk home in the icy snowstorm from Uncle Brian's or you setting up the train around our Christmas tree.

I will always wish I had more time with you, but mostly, I wish you had more time with your son, Joe. Ten days was not enough. But the joy you had on your face the day he was born is something I will always remember and will make sure Joe knows how happy and excited you were to be his Dad. He is so much like you. He is funny, intelligent, kind and loves playing sports. I know you must be very proud of him and of the wonderful mother Kathy has been.

We all miss you very much, and will never understand why you were taken from us so soon. Not a holiday or family party goes by without a thought of you. I'm getting married and, while I know you will be there in spirit with us, it will be your face I will miss seeing in our wedding pictures.

I'm not quite sure how to end this letter because I have so much to say to you. But it will have to wait for now . . . I will love you and miss you every day until we meet again.

Love Always,
Tara

Dear Joe,

A few months ago, Kathy surprised me with a plan of going to Disney World and she invited Jim, Tara and I on the trip. When she told me the planned dates, I explained to her that I had already planned to be off from work that same week! Of course, I was ready to go just hearing her invitation. We left for Disney World on November 16, 2010, the day after your birthday. The trip was just wonderful. As you know, the last time I had been to Disney World was with you and Tara in August, 1983.

This time I would not be going with you, but with Kathy and your son Joe, who is now ten. The word "perfect" does not truly explain the trip. Going on the same rides like Space Mountain and Runaway Train with Joe was almost like having you next to me. He is so much like you . . . his looks, his humor and his love for the fast rides. I got to sit right next to him and we were both screaming our heads off and laughing at the same time while on these fun rides.

I will treasure the memory of this trip with my grandson, as much as I treasure the memory of our trip together.

I want you to know I couldn't have had a better son than you were.

I miss you dearly.

Love,
Mom

Dear Joe,

Well, we just had another family gathering and you were not there. I couldn't help but think of you as I was getting ready and going over the menu. Who was going to bring the shrimp? That was always something you volunteered to do.

I looked around and saw the grandchildren. I know how proud you would be to see your son, Joe. You barely got to hold him but he is so much like you.

I see my daughter—your wife—and I remember how you loved her more than yourself. How you would have done anything for her. I never worried when you asked to marry her. I knew that your love was unfailing.

Our family gatherings will go on, and someone else will bring the shrimp—and when I see it, it will always be you I see and miss and love.

Love,
Ellen

ROBERT T. TWOMEY

Robert T. Twomey was born on September 26, 1952 in Sheepshead Bay, Brooklyn, New York. His parents were Joseph and Helen (Steffens) Twomey. Bob married Marie Harvey in 1972 and they had two sons, Emeric and Robert. He earned a BS from Brooklyn College and attended graduate school at both the University of Georgia and Brooklyn College, working towards a Ph.D. in Cell Biology. Bob loved the biological sciences, English, history, especially American and European History. He was a truly devoted family man and faithful church attendee. Bob loved bike riding, photography and was a naturalist. He worked as a floor broker for Harvey, Young & Yurman on the floor of the Stock Exchange. On Tuesday, September 11, 2001, Bob, his brother-in-law, Emeric Harvey (his employer), along with co-workers were having their weekly Tuesday morning breakfast at Windows on the World on the 107th floor, in the North Tower. He was 48 years old.

Marie (Twomey) Ryan (Wife)
Age: 48

Dear Bob,

At 18, you set out with the dream and desire to be a medical doctor. Having always been a top student, you got discouraged when your grades slipped freshman year at Brooklyn College. You changed majors to Political Science, your second love.

You were almost twenty when we got married. We both agreed that we would wait to start a family so that I would be able to remain home to raise the children. Well, you went to night school for many years, working in a back office on Wall Street, as you switched back to studying your first love, medicine. Your natural ability and proficiency with cameras made using the electron microscope an enjoyment. Your career now had direction. Employed by the New York Zoological Society, you worked in the lab at the N.Y. Aquarium in Coney Island. You went back to school to earn a Ph.D. in cell biology and you earned money by teaching undergrad biology labs.

Then suddenly, we learned that our much dreamed of family was unexpectedly on the way! Thanks be to God!

You decided you would switch gears again, this time from the research to Wall Street. After all, my brother, Ric, had been inviting you to join his company for years. Now that college tuition was a definite future cost, you sacrificed your dream and pursued a more lucrative career in finance. You wanted our children to have the ability to choose colleges without financial limitation. We both always shared the importance of education as #1. The manicured lawn and picket fence were secondary.

We really never could afford vacations beyond the places a car could take us. However, travelling to National Parks as far north as Maine or as far south as the Appalachian Trail in Georgia, was always rewarding. Wherever we were headed, you always seemed to make it a personal guided tour by sharing your vast knowledge of the wildlife, the native birds, the indigenous trees, plants and terrain, even the history of the city we were visiting. The lighthouses we would come upon were also a topic. How you loved photography? It was so natural when you were always ready for moose crossing the road in Maine or the deer that were peeking at us as we approached them on the Appalachian Trail while hiking.

Being an equipment person, you never let us set out to hike, camp or bike ride unless we were all geared up properly. Hiking boots were a must, insect repellant, "waterproof" first aid kit, sunscreen, hats, helmets, Swiss army knife, mini-saw, maps, compass, backpacks and a thermos were considered basics. I always thought it was overkill but was glad to have them as the trip progressed. You were never a Boy Scout but you sure came prepared!

You were an altar boy as a kid in St. Mark's R.C. School, in Sheepshead Bay. Your faith and belief in God always remained with you. The Catholic school education gave you a heart to help others. We used to volunteer at the Methodist Church to feed the homeless and you would stay overnight once a month to help there for a period in time.

We each volunteered to spend one hour a week in the adoration chapel of our church. It was open 24 hours and someone was to always be there. You certainly did your part to try to contribute where and when it could be done. You were very quiet and didn't boast about yourself.

When our two sons came on the scene, you loved getting involved and volunteering as a baseball or basketball coach. As they got older, you were their loyal fan in the bleachers for every practice and game. You actually would forgo taking clients out if our sons had an important event going on. You thankfully had your priorities right. It was never about self-promotion or money but always about our family.

I was always touched by something said to me by one of the men who knew you on the AMEX Floor. He told me that you always referred to me as your best friend. What a shock. You never said this to me and I was so heartened to hear it that I honestly thought the guy who told me it was just trying to say this to make me feel good. Once confirmed, I have to say hearing it was like receiving a priceless gift. It really filled my heart with love.

Some years after 9/11, I received two CDs from the City of New York containing your last phone calls to the emergency 911 operator. I had no idea that you ever made any phone calls. In fact, few civilians did. Oh, just to hear your voice again was wonderful yet heartbreaking. I see God's hand in this as a way of showing His faithfulness even through the evil things that befall us from this world.

On the calls, you ask for permission or advice regarding the breaking of the glass windows up there. Was it advisable to do so? You were in the restaurant, Windows on the World, on the 107th floor. Being science oriented, you were concerned if the oxygen would exacerbate the situation. You continued to say how there were pregnant women up there with you and the smoke situation was getting worse by the second. You called the 911 operator three times trying to get an answer from them. You sounded urgent, concerned and frustrated but amazingly calm. However, no answer was forthcoming. The phone call got cutoff.

I realized why God had me receive this CD. The Lord wanted us to see how, in your last moments of life, you followed your heart's true desire to care for others. Hence, your first love and desire to be a doctor. You actually ended your life concerned for these pregnant women. I could just see you trying to make them comfortable, giving your jacket to cover them, trying to diminish smoke inhalation. In your final moments, it is evident you were truly a hero! The smoke apparently overcame you and I am sure you all fell into a sleep. This confirms the way I envisioned your final moments from the beginning. God gifted me with this confirmation.

In March of 2002, we received notification that your body was found. I thought they were being politically correct but your clothing, down to your boxer shorts, and loose dollar bills in your pocket, were found!

I remain grateful for the 29 years of life we had together and for the closure of having you found. A definite miracle. You would truly be rewarded to know how our two sons forged ahead through these difficult times to complete degrees at Fordham University and the University of Georgia and one is currently attending Emory Law School. Both are carving out good lives. You were a good role model and a loving man, father and husband.

I miss you, my love.

Marie

MATTHEW J. GRZYMALSKI

Matthew J. Grzymalski was born on February 21, 1967 in Brooklyn, New York to Patricia and Joseph Grzymalski of New Hyde Park, New York. Matthew enjoyed playing golf, the New York Giants, his nieces and nephews and spending time on the east end of Long Island with his friends. Matthew worked on the 105th Floor of One World Trade Center for Cantor Fitzgerald. His girlfriend, Kaleen Pezzuti, also of Cantor, worked with Matthew at the same trading desk and were presumably together there when they passed on September 11th. He was 34 years old.

Patti Ann Grzymalski Valerio (Sister)
Age: 50

Dear Matthew,

I can't believe how much time has gone by since we last saw you. Our anniversary trip to Ground Zero is never easy. Although you are not here physically, I can say that I do feel your presence around me. Whenever a Van Morrison song comes on, it is your face that I see.

There are so many things that trigger memories of you. I still have the shorts that you wore when you jumped in my pool the weekend we celebrated Thomas' birthday here at my house in August 2001. It feels as though it was yesterday. I am so sad that my children, Thomas, James and Kelly, are not able to grow up knowing their Uncle Matt. Since you and Kaleen had gotten so close, we were sure that there would be another Grzymalski wedding and, hopefully, another cousin eventually.

Your nephew, Thomas, celebrated his 17th birthday and is about to graduate high school. Of course, most of the talk is about college—well, I am the one doing most of the talking! He has become a very busy athlete. Currently, he is on two soccer teams and already the basketball season seems to be starting and it is only September. He has his learner's permit and drives every chance he gets (when he is actually home). He is a great kid and you would be so proud of him. Of course, he plays baseball, too. I am sure you can't forget all the Whiffle ball games we played in our backyard on Morris Drive. He is definitely a big sports fan, always catching up on all the scores. He gets up early for school and makes sure to save time to watch "SportsCenter" on ESPN. On Sundays during football season, he goes to Monaghans in Rockville Centre with our brothers, Paul and Joe, to eat wings, drink (soda!) and, of course, watch the Jets. Even though the Mets are, once again, NOT in the World Series, he'll be a Mets fan forever! He is contemplating becoming a physical education teacher.

Your godson, James, is now fifteen. If you were here, I think you would agree how much he resembles our family. He even has the Grzymalski temperament! James is also an athlete. He plays baseball (pitches) and is on a travel team three seasons out of the year. We even take vacations with his team—baseball tournaments out of state. But his favorite sport, like his older brother, is basketball. Thomas is on varsity and James on junior varsity. He does have a very sensitive side and can read between the lines. James can tell when something is bothering me. He can tell when I need a hug and always obliges. He also notices things that nobody else does. For example, if I get my hair cut or if it looks a little blonder than it did the day before, he will say something. Mom always says that you were always so observant, too. James just finished ninth grade and he is very popular. Everyone knows him and likes him, especially the girls. One of James' favorite things to do is to play video games. Thanks to the internet, he can play versus his friends online. James does not have any idea what he would like to be when he is older. I keep mentioning the Coast Guard. He loves the water and loves to swim. On a camping trip one summer several years ago, we rafted down the Delaware—but James swam almost the entire distance! Two things both of my boys are good at are eating and snowboarding. They truly enjoy each other's company. They are still growing—they are way taller than me and will probably pass their Dad in height. Thomas and James are already great friends and I am so glad. They have the same type of relationship you had with our brothers and JoAnn and myself.

Kelly is every bit the athlete that her brothers are. She is thirteen years old and in the seventh grade. The last time I heard your voice was on my telephone answering machine. You had left a message asking me how Kelly's first day of nursery school was. She was three. But don't worry—just because she was so little when you died does not mean she does not know you. She remembers our Dad taking her in the stroller for a walk around the block and she was 2 ½ when he died. We always talk about you and Dad. She has seen tons of pictures and has heard all the stories. I tell her how Dad would volunteer you to follow me to make sure I got home safely with my babies when Joe was working at the firehouse at night. Kelly is really into soccer. She has been playing since she has been four (just like her big brother, Thomas) and she is good. She is one of the goal scorers on her team. We travel, too, with her team for out-of-state soccer tournaments. She also likes to play basketball and softball. She always does well at school and this year she is in all honors classes. She is very diligent with her homework and school projects. She always goes above and beyond. She is already talking about becoming a teacher! Last year, she was in the middle school play and even had a solo at the spring concert. Kelly is my right hand. We are very close. She is very in tune to my moods and always wants to help me with whatever I am doing. I am very lucky to have my little girl. She is very close to Uncle Paul and Uncle Joe and, of course, to Mom.

One of my favorite memories is from our family vacations to Wyler's Lake in Pennsylvania. When Thomas was little I wanted to ensure that he would have the same type of fond memories from his vacations as we did. We go to Myrtle Beach every year. Both of the boys play golf and this past summer, Kelly even played nine holes with Joe. She loved it. Mom usually comes with us to Myrtle Beach. Peter loved it so much, he actually moved down there with Lenore and the kids. We used to stay in the condo that you bought with Mom and our brother, Joe, until she bought the new townhouse alongside the golf course. Mom takes the kids right out the back door to practice golf. Some of your golf shirts are hanging in the closet and when my husband, Joe, plays golf, he uses Dad's golf clubs. We have created great memories from our time there.

JoAnn, Bill, Ryan and Liam are doing great, as is Paul and his son, Matthew—we call him Baci. Our brother, Joe, is still operating Dad's business, Garden City Printers & Mailers. Paul is working there, too. Last year, Mom sold our family house on Morris Drive in New Hyde Park and moved to a really nice townhouse development. She has lots of friends and is very busy. You would be so proud of Mom. She is very strong and she is a role model for me. She just returned from a two-week trip to Alaska. Paul and Joe come over often and we have fun sitting in my yard around the chiminea (even in the winter).

Matty, we miss you and Daddy so much. You can be sure that you are always remembered. Please continue to watch over all of us until we see you again.

Love your sister,
Patti Ann

WILLIAM V. STECKMAN

William Steckman was born December 24, 1944 in New York City to Vincent and Mildred Steckman. He had a sister, Janet, whom he adored. He was married to Barbara Steckman with whom he had five children (Donna, Debbie, Deanine, Diana, and Billy). William enjoyed boating, family vacations, tinkering around the garage and operating a Ham radio which he was trained to do in the US Coast Guard. He worked at NBC since 1967 where he was a transmitter engineer. On September 11, 2001, he was just finishing up his night shift in a room full of 10,000 watt equipment on the 104th floor of one World Trade Center just below the needle. He was 56.

Diana Devito (Daughter)
Age: 35

Dear Dad,

With your big brown eyes and dark brown hair, your smile would light up a room. You were such an amazing person in every way possible.

You were 56 when we lost you on 9/11, and for thirty-five of your years, you devoted yourself to your job at NBC as a transmitter engineer. Like many others, you should not have been in the Towers when tragedy hit. You were a dedicated employee as well as a fun loving family man. You married your high school sweetheart and raised five of us in a loving home. You were able to spend quality time with the grandkids doing fun and exciting things with them: from making a handmade ice skating rink in the back yard to watching movies and acting them out; from hand making characters from their favorite movies to just having long talks. They would get lost in a "magical basement" with their Pop-Pop. It was as if no one else was around. Their faces light up as they yelled "Pop-Pop".

You could always make us smile with your sense of humor and you were well known for cracking little jokes or reciting funny lines from movies. Your sense of humor brought lots of joy to our family. You were a big family man, from backyard BBQs to birthdays and holidays, you ALWAYS wanted the family to be together. Together is where we all were on that tragic day. Together waiting to hear that someone saw you or that you are on your way home or even that you are hurt but alive. But nothing. So together we stood by each other as best as we could to mourn you and to deal with our very public grief.

Now, almost ten years later, I am proud to say that I did get through this terrible tragedy and even though at times it tears me up inside, I learned that even on some of the darkest days of my life, the sun will shine. Some days, it is a little brighter than others; some days will be as dark as that September day.

Dad, I think when someone grieves a loved one they have to find what they need personally to help get through it. The kids remember you finding a starfish on the beach while out on your boat. I Googled "starfish" and found this story

A man walks along a beach where there are hundreds of starfish going to suffer out of the water. He tries to save them by picking them up, one by one, and throwing them back into the water. A stranger yells to him, "It won't make a difference, you can't save them all." But the man continued throwing them back into the ocean's setting sun and with deep compassion said, "I made a difference to *that* one."

You certainly made a difference in my life and I have to believe that you helped people get out of the building that day. You did make a difference to someone and, because of your loving compassionate ways, I am the person that I am today because of you.

Love Always,
Diana

THOMAS FITZPATRICK

Thomas James Fitzpatrick was born on October 24th, 1965 in the Bronx, New York to Michael and Roseanna Fitzpatrick, and was the brother of Michael. He married Marianna Pennino in 1994 and they have two children, Brendan and Caralyn. Thomas earned a BA from Boston College, an MBA from Fordham and his CPA certificate before changing occupations to a financial advisor at Sandler O'Neill. Thomas loved his family and many friends, Boston College and playing golf. On September 11th, Thomas was at his desk on the 104th floor of the Southern Tower. He was 35 years old.

Mike Fitzpatrick (Father)
Age: 73

Roseanna Fitzpatrick (Mother)
Ages: 70

Marianne Fitzpatrick (Wife)
Age: 45

Dear Thomas,

We are moving over the Triboro Bridge in a frantic drive,
Our little boy was almost ready to arrive.
His Mother's water had broken and she told me birth was near,
I told her squeamishly, "Don't worry I'm here".
Thirty five years, ten months and eighteen days until September
    Eleven
Today our little boy is playing golf up in heaven.
We thought it might be fun to review your short life span,
So lend us your ear for a minute if you can.

We took you home from the hospital all full of fun and frolic,
Whoever thought the lousy kid would be colic.
While your one year-old brother Michael slept like a lamb,
Your constant crying sounded like a twelve-piece band.
Six years passed like the blink of an eye,
And off to your kindergarten play went his Mother and I.
You were dressed like a lion tamer,
Ready to step into his cage,

Then the whole audience noticed
That you had forgotten your whip backstage.
So you went through the motions without whip in hand,
And after you finished everybody began to clap and stand.

On to Fordham Prep you would go,
And your parents were so proud as you continued to grow.
Four years later with all your new found knowledge,
You took our old Chevy to register at Boston College.
Most of your Boston College Eagle buddies are here today at
    this Mass
Reminiscing of dorm parties, exam cramming and the Doug
    Flutie pass.
Your graduation from Boston College was an unforgettable event,
You soon became a CPA but a salesman on Wall Street was your
    real bent.
You chose a spectacular little woman, Marianne, for your wife,
And not long thereafter, little Brendan and Caralyn graced your
    life.

Rarely did a day go by that you didn't give Mom a ring,
To talk about the broken boiler, backed-up toilet or some other
    silly thing.
So in closing, thanks Thomas, for being a Wonderful Son,
You've filled our Lives with Meaning and Unforgettable Fun.
And when Mom and Dad take the same escalator as you,
Please give Mom a kiss,
And for Dad, a Tee Time or Two.

Love Mom & Dad

Dear Thomas,

It has been so long since I have written to you. The years have flown by and so much has happened. Brendan has grown from an adorable two year-old, into a handsome, intelligent young man, who reminds me of you every day. It amazes me how he can have so many of your facial expressions, your sense of humor and your mischievous ways. Our little four month-old, Caralyn, has become a beautiful young lady, with your temperament and outgoing personality. She loves to sing and dance, but thankfully has my rhythm and not yours! The children are your gift to me that I cherish every day, and I am glad that I can see your traits in them. We speak of you a lot and your pictures around the house remind us of your love and your life with us.

Thankfully your parents have remained in our lives and we love visiting with Grandpa Mike, aka "Meatball" and Grandma Roseanne, aka "Spaghetti". The kids love Grandpa's stories and I am grateful they are always there for us. We often spend time with your brother and his family too, despite his love for Notre Dame!

As for me, I still miss you, my love, and I often think about how our life would have been a happy one. September 11th was a day that changed my life forever and, for a while, I didn't know if I could recover. We had been together for 22 years and I had to become a stronger, more independent person without you to lean on. Our family and friends were so helpful and without them I might not have made it through some days (especially when both kids were in diapers). There were so many caring people in the world and through a Tuckahoe bereavement group, I met a special friend. She also lost her husband on 9/11 and had a three year-old son. Our families have shared many happy and sad moments over the years and I am glad they are in our lives. She helped me get through the deaths of my grandmother and my Dad, with whom I hope you are sharing in our special moments. I have also been lucky enough to find love again. Joe has joined our family and has been wonderful in many ways. He loves the children as his own and is involved in all aspects of their lives. He has shown me that I could be happy again and have a new family life.

I know you would be happy that I am teaching at a preschool and that I love it. I have also gotten very involved in the kids' school and have become PTA co-president. I am also on the Family Advisory Board of Tuesday's Children, which is a terrific September 11th charity. They have done so much for our family and others, including first responders.

Our lives are busy, but happy, and I think that you would be proud of the family we have become. Know that we love you and that we continue to honor you every day of our lives.

Until we meet again,
Love you always,
Marianne

MICHAEL BRADLEY FINNEGAN

Michael Bradley Finnegan was born on March 14, 1964 in Syracuse, New York, to Frank and Beverly Finnegan, the brother of Katherine. He married Erin McDonnell in 1992 and they have three children, Bridget, Bradley and Jack, who was born on August 3rd, 2001. Michael earned a BA in Economics from the University of Richmond in 1986. He started working on Wall Street as a currency broker and eventually ended up at Cantor Fitzgerald. Mike loved his wife, three children and a very large, extended group of family and friends. Mike was an excellent golfer, won his club championship twice, and loved the game. On September 11th, 2001, he was at his desk on the 104th Floor of the North Tower in the Northwest corner of the building. He was 37 years old.

Frank and Beverly Finnegan (Parents)
Ages: 71, 65

Jeffrey W. Craig (Friend)
Age: 47

Katherine Finnegan (sister)
Age: 48

Dear Mike:

We miss you terribly and think about you every day. We remember . . .

One night, long after your curfew, Dad stood waiting in the kitchen for you to slink in the house. He grabbed you by the collar and raised you about three inches off the floor and stood nose-to-nose and screamed, "Where the hell have you been?" You blinked and blurted out, "I was parking with my date."

Mom was at the stairs and cracked up, laughing. Dad just shook his head and sent you to bed. You always had a difficult time telling a lie.

We remember when you were 15 or so, you were swimming at the club pool after a day of golf, and the General Manager came over to the pool and asked if there were any kids who could drive. Apparently, there was a private party that night and the valet parking team hadn't show up. You responded and organized a team to park the cars, much to the relief of the GM. You parked a Bentley, remember? When all guests had arrived and were seated in the dining room, you pulled the Bentley up to the pool and invited a dozen of the younger kids for a ride down the street to Friendly's for ice cream. We didn't learn about your little excursion until after 9/11, when a young lady from the pool snack bar sent us a letter.

We remember when you won the Ulster County Men's Amateur Golf Championship your senior year of high school, at the time, the youngest winner in history. On the last hole of the stroke play tournament, you teed off into a 30-mph headwind, to a green that was over the horizon, and out of sight. Dad was caddying for you. You hit a four-iron for your approach, with the tip of the flag providing a target. There was a crowd walking up the last fairway with us. Our club pro came down the hill, and said to you, "If you can get up and down from there, you win". Now the green was still completely out of sight, and where your ball was relative to the pin was unknown. I'll never forget the look in your eyes, and your response. "I can get up and down from there!" And, of course, you did.

We remember when you got engaged to Erin. You were Christmas shopping at the Short Hills Mall. We remember you relayed to us how you had suggested Erin get in line to see Santa Claus, and when it was her turn, Santa asked her name. Erin identified herself, Santa said that he had something for her and he gave her a gift wrap box. Sure enough, you had put the ring in it and the rest is history.

Mike, one of our neighbors commented that while many neighbors were friendly and waved hello as they drove by, you would frequently stop, get out of your car and talk. You would always be able to recall something that was going on with a neighbor's family, and ask for an update.

Your father-son bond was remarkable. You called Dad almost every day to tell him the latest joke or just to touch base.

Sometimes, you called Dad from home and ask him to turn on the TV to watch a tournament together, and you would talk through the tournament. Dad was so honored to be your best man at your wedding.

We remember how competitive you always were (in a good way) with your sister, Katherine. She would call you and say, 'Wasn't it nice to receive a generous check from Mom and Dad? Oh, you didn't get one?' You called Katherine when it was below zero in New York, and tell her that you were in a limo, someplace warm, picking up some customers for golf. As time went on and you both married and started families, you shared the experiences of parenthood.

You always loved to talk to others about the latest swing technique that you found useful in golf, and share it with whoever was interested. You always encouraged your friends, exhorting them to hang in there—that they could break par or do whatever was necessary to win.

We love the story of when you and Erin were skiing in Colorado with another couple. You were in a restaurant having a great time, and you had a small camera, and you turned to an adjacent table and motioned with the camera. The person who you motioned to was a very big Hollywood star. The star said sure, and started to pose, you handed him the camera and motioned to the star to take the picture. The star loved it.

Love,
Mom and Dad

Dear Michael,

Unfortunately for those closely connected to the events of September 11, 2001, Heaven is a place that we have become all too familiar with at too young of an age. However, a look to the sky brings all our loved ones down to earth. It brings the heavens close enough to touch, the angels close enough to hear us speak, pray and finish the tales and stories that those of us still on earth did not have the opportunity to hear or tell. These very same conversations hurt and heal with varied emotions that allow for the passage of time to patch the broken hearts.

Nary has a day passed that I don't look to the sky in search of council, advice, prayers and loving wishes from the best friend who always had words to sooth and direct. I never have to look very far to see your face in the shape of a cloud, that smiles upon life on earth. This image blesses me with happiness, motivation, a prayer and good wishes that make the day brighter by far. The message arms me with faith and confidence to be strong, kind and to live life with enthusiasm and love. The little things in life seem to take a back seat to those that matter most.

The faces in the clouds are a living reminder that you are always with us and that the families, spouses and children are blessed and are watched over every minute of every day. As life challenges us to be patient until we are united again, it does let all those on earth know that we do not wander without love and cause. We shall make each day more fulfilling than the last and treasure friends, family and memories until we meet again in the place that we learned of too soon—Heaven.

Yes, Heaven is a place on earth where love, laughter and memories stimulate confidence in loved ones that have been left on the waiting list to be oh so patient until our time is called. Since that time, many have been sent to see you with messages of love and loss to the place where we will all once meet again.

For those who have earned their place in heaven, think not of what you have left behind but what you have empowered us to do in your spirit until we meet again.

God bless you, Michael Bradley "Finny" Finnegan. Please know that Erin, Bridget, Bradley and Jack wait patiently until the Heavens come to earth. Thank you for a life of fondness and admiration, fulfillment and for my love of Christ. I trust that I have honored you proudly with faith and actions, as you would your best friend.

God Bless,
Jeffrey W. Craig

Dear Michael,

I often wonder what you are doing and what you would think of us today. As ten years approach since you've been gone, we have grown, matured, and forgiven.

Our family is intact. Mom and Dad look past their sadness to see the joy in front of them. Our anger, for years, loomed, but it's gone now. Time, the great healer, (just don't tell a mourner), has come through. And, while sadness can peak in at any moment with no warning, I think there is a place in a happy life to have sadness once in a while. Life is good. We have not become victims of the senselessness of everything about that day; how foolish it would be to dwell on its effect. Life is what we have, and you are alive in us.

Your children are you, in every way. I attribute this to Erin's eternal love for you, and Mom and Dad's strength and commitment to family. The support your family has received is the most incredible thing; from people who love you to people you never knew. There is good everywhere. Bridget is beautiful from the inside out. She is perfect, like you always said. One look at Bradley is like seeing you. His glance conveys understanding. Jack is a gift to all of us. If I had one wish, it would be for you to have a few minutes with each of them, right when they needed it the most in their lives.

I want to believe you are there, somewhere, but my guess is, the trials of this world, look a bit insignificant from where you are. I want to share a long family beach walk with you, just like we did on our vacations, where time just stands still and the awesomeness of the night sky and the ocean fill our breath.

I miss you, but you are here, when I need you.

I love you, Kath

KHANG N. NGUYEN

Khang Ngoc Nguyen was born on December 19, 1959 in Saigon, Vietnam. He was one of nine children born to Bich and Quy Nguyen. He and his entire family came to America in 1981. Khang married Tu HoNguyen on July 4, 1993 and they have one son, An Ho-Ngoc Nguyen. Khang graduated with a BS degree in Electrical Engineering from the University of Maryland and was just short a few hours from earning a Master's Degree from George Mason University. He worked for Science Applications International Corporation (SAIC) and was assigned to work as a Systems Administrator at the Navy Command Center in the Pentagon. He loved his family, playing soccer, tennis, and had a passion for playing guitar. On September 11th, Khang was in his office on the second floor of D Ring in the Pentagon. He was 41 years old.

Annie HoNguyen (Sister-in-Law)
Age: 44

Dear Khang,

As each hour of each day inched by, even the slimmest hope of your safe homecoming began to vanish. You were forever gone, leaving behind the tremendous pains and remembrance in every one of us.

In your family, you were the eldest son. In my family, you were the eldest son-in-law. From the day you became a member of our family till the day we last saw you, you had always been successful in his "big brother" role. My husband and I have always loved and respected you as our own blood brother. You were generous, kindhearted, and modest. You were kind in your thoughts, words, and actions. Within your ability, you would try your best to please and attend to the needs of everyone. From every business trip, you always brought home suitcases full of gifts for everyone. For any occasions, all of us could expect to receive "an anonymous present" from you. You didn't concern much for the thank-you letters or the appreciative compliments. You would just be as satisfied if you could make us content.

You loved sports and had a passion for music. Your "idol" was singer Vu-Khanh. You owned each and every tape, CD, and album that featured Vu-Khanh. There was not a love song Vu-Khanh sang that you didn't know by heart. After the birth of An, you and Tu's only son, you taught yourself a variety of children's songs, in Vietnamese, in English, and in other foreign languages. With little An sitting on your lap, you played the guitar and sang to your son. Taking after his Dad, baby An knew how to sing before saying his first word. He mimicked and sang along to any song, at the right rhythms, even if he had just heard it once.

Of all my nieces and nephews, An had been the child owning the largest possession of toys. Almost every day, coming home from work, you would purchase some kind of toy for your son.

When An was younger, you liked to buy balls for him. An owns all kinds of balls, in various sizes and colors. When An grew older, you bought him tons of educational toys, either in the forms of the alphabets, numbers, picture books, or cartoon videotapes. Little An enjoys putting the alphabets together to make up words. Every time An finished forming a word or accomplished any task, you clapped your hands in joy and praised An in your satisfactorily half-laughing voice: "Good job, An. Very good job!"

My Mom still recalls the experience on An's birthday, the 9th of September, two days before you were declared missing. You kept following your birthday son around and asked, "How old are you, An?" Little An, in the past twelve months, had been so used to answer "Three years old", that on that day, he had to be taught to change his answer to, "An is four-years-old". After a bit of hesitation, he doubtfully said, "An is four years-old" and put up his four little fingers. Just like that, father and son: one asked, the other answered for almost the entire day. And every time An gave the correct answer, you clapped your hands, said in joy, "An is good, so good", again and again . . .

The normally active and carefree little An has now turned "heart-brokenly" quiet. At the school playground or at home, he sometimes can be spotted withdrawing to a corner, isolating himself from everyone else. He cares less about friends, toys, and even the TV cartoon shows that he used to enjoy watching so much. He doesn't say a word, nor pays attention to anybody. He just sits quietly by himself. Each of us in our family, either seeing him in that state with our own eyes or hearing it from others, feels like our own heart is being stabbed with a sharp knife. My poor little nephew An! His immature comprehension and limited vocabulary is not helping him express his sorrow. Alone, he grieves in his own way. When he withdraws to his own world, we understand, the heart of the little child is longing for his dear Daddy. Tragic as it may be, An will never comprehend for a long time why Daddy has not come home for him. He will not fully grasp why Daddy has not returned home to hold him in his arms, put him on his lap, teach him new songs, or bring him to Chuck E. Cheese on the weekends. An also does not understand why his Mommy, lately, cries all the times. When his mother cries, An hurriedly runs to grab a tissue to wipe the tears off her eyes. He holds his mother's hands, shakes them and nervously begs: "Mommy, don't cry. I'm sorry, Mommy." The innocent words of the young child not only couldn't stop his Mommy from crying further but also makes her heart ache even more.

Since then, little An has been no longer having chance to stand on his chair, peeking through the window curtains, and waiting for you to come home from work, as he used to do every evening. Instead, An has learned how to bow in front of your shrine to say good-bye to you prior to leaving for school, greeting you when coming home, or blowing a goodnight kiss to you before going to bed.

Each day, at dinner time, looking at my nephew putting his two small hands together in front of his chest, standing straight in front of your shrine, bowing a few times before saying: "Daddy, please join us for dinner", I still hear the echo of your joyous voice saying with pride: "An is my best!"

Love,
Annie

MICHAEL STABILE

Michael F. Stabile was born on January 11, 1951, in Brooklyn, New York to Anna and Carl Stabile; he was the brother of Lucille, Richard, Carol and John. Michael married Roseanna Giambrone in 1973 and they have three children: Michele, Robert, and Lauren. Mike worked for Euro Brokers on and off for years, returning to the company in 1997 until his death in 2001. Mike loved spending time with his wife and children and coached many of his children's sports teams when they were growing up. Mike liked going to Atlantic City and rooting for his two favorite teams, the New York Mets and the New York Jets. On September 11th, Mike was leaving the 84th floor of the South Tower. He was 50 years old.

Michele Stabile (Daughter)
Age: 32

Dear Dad,

Did you ever realize that as you get older, memories from the past tend to fade? That only some memories stay in your mind? And certain songs trigger these memories?

I have one about you that doesn't go away the older I get, and I'm truly grateful for that. You always made us listen to two radio stations: WFAN during baseball season and CBS FM, which, at the time, played oldies from the 50s to the early 80s. I don't know the exact year the song came out or exactly how old I was. We were in the car and you were singing to me; it was the Lionel Richie song "You Are".

Growing up, I didn't much think about the meaning of the song and why you were singing it to me. It had all become clear when I was in my freshman year of college. You had written me a letter (which I have since lost) saying that you and Mom tried for so long to have a child. You made a pact with God that if you went back to Church every week, would God bless them with a baby? Well, wouldn't you know, your prayers were answered and not long after that, Mom became pregnant with me.

The next time I heard the song, I thought back to when I was that little girl and you were singing to me in the car. The words of the song are special and I realized that you loved me more than anything in the world. I am sure you and Mom my felt the same way about my siblings. But I know that when I hear that song, you are looking down on me. You made a special song request and somehow, somewhere, it was answered.

Love,
Michele

YUDH V. S. JAIN

Yudh V. S. Jain was born in 1947 in India. In the late 1960s, he came to the United States to pursue his Ph.D. at the University of Nebraska, Lincoln. A few years later, he and his wife, Sneh, settled in the New York Tri-State area, raising their two daughters, Sargam (Mona) and Vandna (Cheena). Yudh worked for over 25 years as an engineer, travelling across the globe, until he began working for Cantor Fitzgerald/E-Speed. He was a true gentleman and treated all with respect and kindness. He was passionate about continuing to learn, spending time with his family, enjoying photography, and making people happy. On September 11, 2011, he was on the 103rd Floor of the North Tower. He was 54 years old.

Vandna Cheena Jain (Daughter)
Age: 27

Dear Dad,

I wanted to share pieces of the letters I've written to you over the years.

September 2003:

There is no greater gift to give to you than to live for you. So thank you for giving me my life. I love you and I hope you are happy wherever you may be.

July 2009:

I bought a book on Indian Spirituality today and while I was reading it and understanding more about Hinduism and Jainism, etc. I realized that based on our faith, the likelihood that I'll really see you again, in another life, in heaven, is pretty slim. It's not that you won't be there, but I'm not sure we'll really recognize each other. I mean, I suppose in the end, our souls continue on, with our bodies being vessels during our lifetimes. So I suppose I am trying my hardest to believe that a piece of your soul is in me. I've really started recognizing parts of you that have become parts of me.

When I was in India, I saw Babli Bua and she looked at me and said that I looked so much like you. She said that I reminded her of you and that she missed you so much. I told her I didn't think I looked like you, which I realized later was totally inaccurate on my part.

Someone asked me the other day what a Chikku was. I gave them half a response, but I remembered that you used to call me that as a nickname and all of a sudden I really missed it. Sometimes I can remember the sound of your voice; it's like a blurred, faded memory which I don't want to forget. I wish I could have one of our long conversations like we used to, where I talked most of the time.

November 2006:

Just yesterday someone at work was talking about Scientology and how weird it is. And we looked up what an "E-meter" was and I don't know I realized I really missed testing batteries with you. People normally don't test batteries to see if they'll still work. But you did and it was something different that I don't think anyone I'll ever meet would think to do. I thought of that and I realized how long it was since I had even tested a AA battery with you. It's such a simple, almost pointless activity and most people wouldn't even bother storing that little voltage tester of yours. But I wanted to go home and just use it. I mean, am I insane? I used to do everything with you, even test batteries and now I can't even do that.

November 2009:

You weren't here for my 26th birthday two weeks ago. I have thought about you a lot. I was a bit sad that Sunday, so I kept to myself like I have for the past few years. Can you believe I am 26 now? Last time you saw me was when I was 17! I wonder if I would look very different to you now? I'll be 30 soon, isn't that nuts?

And then there's all that stuff in the news about the trials of those people. I don't want to upset you, but Dad, I know you. You wouldn't wish them death, you don't have it in you. I can't believe that they will have the trial in NYC. And I don't know how I feel. I want them to answer to what they have done. I do want to see the people who helped take you away. But Dad, I promise not to hate them, because to hate them means to give in to ideology that led them to do what they did.

You know we went to the memorial and Sis is usually pretty regular. She doesn't get upset or cry. But we went to the memorial concert and I remember the singer had one lyric that went: "Tuesday came and went, went one September, when will she come again? The thing about memories is that they are sure and bound to fade. Except for the stolen souls left on her blade. Is Monday coming back?" And I never have seen Sis cry so hard. She just all of a sudden started crying so badly and I had to get her a tissue. I know she misses you a lot too, Dad. She gets teary sometimes. I see it in her eyes.

For a long time, Dad, I just didn't understand us. You know, Mom, Sis, you and me. Even when you were here. It still doesn't make sense, but I suppose I have a sense of respect, recognition and an odd sense of pride about it all. I've learned so much about you and Mom and India, stories from before and during my existence. And it just enriches me as a human being. I know I'm still flawed, but I find it ever so moving that I can still learn so much about you even though you're not here and that I can love you even more than before.

January 2010:

Things are not perfect here, but you know I'm still trying to find the good from what happened that day. I'm learning to be a better daughter, I think. I'm learning to be a better person, maybe. I'm recognizing the parts of you and the parts of Mom, the Indian and the American bits of myself. Maybe I'm a little more patient. And this year has been so hard, with Mom being sick and just everything, but we're managing it. Yet, it didn't surprise me. We've grown so much as a family.

December 2010:

In a several months it will be ten years since you've been gone. And guess what? Sis is getting married. She got engaged just a couple of months ago. Her fiancé is a wonderful person. We're all so happy for them. I keep thinking about that pagadi I bought you. Who knew that when I bought it for you in August ten years ago, that almost exactly ten years later, we'd have the occasion for you to wear it.

I'll never forget what our friend David Kwoh wrote once:

Last time I saw Yudh, it was two days before the WTC attack. As I said goodbye, he said that we would get together again. How I wish I could give him a big hug for that final farewell. My friend, keep your promise and meet me in my dreams.

Dad, the last time I saw you, you were dropping me off at the dorms in college. Months before, you wondered if I would call you often when I finally left home. And on the morning of September 11, 2001, as the attacks occurred, I, unaware, was picking up the package you had sent me. Even to the last hour, you were there for me. I don't often see you in my dreams, but when I do, I always fail to save you from tragic circumstances. So Daddy, one day soon, come visit me and tell me that you're okay. Then we can sit somewhere and you can be my sweet, loving, caring father once again.

With love from your dear, darling daughter,

Cheena

DAVID S. LEE

David S. Lee was born on August 11, 1964 in Brooklyn, New York to Watson and Siu-Lan Lee. He married Angela in 2000 and was expecting his first child in 2002. David earned a BA from Wharton and an MBA from the Kellogg School of Management. He was a devoted Yankees fan, loved to play golf and looked forward to fatherhood. David worked at Fiduciary Trust International and on September 11, he was on the 94th floor of the South Tower. He was 37 years old.

Ryan Lee (Son)
Age: 9

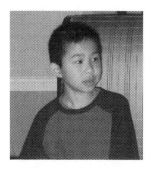

Dear Daddy,

I'm a boy and my name is Ryan. I like to play baseball, golf and tennis. My favorite major league team is the Mets. Whenever I can, I watch the Mets play. I love to watch Star Wars and The Clone Wars. My hobby is building Legos.

I love to go to Cape May, as you did with Mommy. I love dinosaurs and reading about them. Uncle Dennis gave me a Wii for Christmas and I love to play Wii with my friends. Mommy also enjoys playing Mario with me. I love to read, especially mysteries.

Daddy, I wish you were here so you can play ball with me. In the meantime, Uncle Charlsen has been teaching me the basics. Someday, I would like to be a professional baseball player. Maybe, I will be drafted while in high school, but Mommy said I have to go to college first. For now, I have a lot of practice to do.

Love,
Ryan

FRANK BONOMO

Frank J. Bonomo was born on August 12th, 1959 to Katherine and Joseph Bonomo in Queens, New York, the brother of Lenore. He married Margarite Bonomo on September 24th, 1994. Frank loved his job as a NYC Firefighter and was on the job for 17 years as of September 11th. He loved his wife and children (Joseph and Juliana who were only 4 and 1 at the time of September 11th). He was an avid Jets and Mets fan and loved to play golf. He died a hero trying to save others. He was 42 years old.

Juliana (Daughter)
Age: 11

Joseph (Son)
Age: 14

Dear Daddy Frank,

I know I can't see you, but I know you can see me. I know you are always watching down on me. I am having a great time and I hope you are too, somewhere in that bright blue heaven. I LOVE you and MISS you lots.

Xoxoxoxoxoxoxoxoxoxoxox

Happy Birthday!!!

Love your daughter . . . Juliana

P.S. Can I see you one last time, please?

Frank, My Daddy

I remember you took me for an Italian ice after I finished my whole dinner. One time you took me when I didn't even finish my dinner. You took me to Chuck-E-Cheese with some of my friends. You used to love it when I made pictures at school. You were a firefighter who saved all the people after the building collapsed. You died in heaven cause that is where you wanted to be. You love to be in heaven cause it doesn't cost any money. You can get any soda you want from the soda machine. You died like Billy Blazer, a Rescue Hero. I love you.

Love,
Joseph

MARK SCOTT ZEPLIN

Marc Scott Zeplin was born on February 12, 1968 in Oceanside, Long Island. He was the son of Leona and Leonard Zeplin and brother of Joslin Zeplin. He married Debra Rosenberg in October of 1996. Mark became the father of Ryan Harris Zeplin in September of 1998 and Ethan Gabriel Zeplin in December 2000. He earned a BA in Political Science with honors from the University of Michigan in 1990and earned an MBA in 1993 from the University of Michigan Business School. Mark worked for Cantor Fitzgerald as an equities trader. He loved his children greatly and truly enjoyed his time with them. He also enjoyed watching and playing sports, especially hockey. He was a "true blue" Rangers fan. On September 11th, Marc was on the 104th floor of the North Tower. He was 33 years old.

Debra Zeplin (Wife)
Age: 34

Leona Zeplin (Mother)

Joslin Zeplin-Paradise (Sister)

Dear Marc,

I can't believe that it is almost 10 years since you died. I think about you every day and miss you greatly. You were the most wonderful person and I have such great memories of our life together. I'll never forget the day I met you. I opened my apartment door when you showed up for our blind date in February 1995, and from the minute I met you, I knew that I would fall in love with you and you would be the man that I would marry. We went to a Rangers hockey game and our blind date lasted an entire weekend, and we saw each other every day from then on. A year later, you proposed to me in a helicopter over the Statue of Liberty, coincidentally with the World Trade Center towers in the background. You then had a limo waiting (with a dozen roses and a bottle of champagne) which took us to Café des Artistes for our engagement dinner. You were truly a romantic. You were always full of surprises, and did everything you could to make all of our experiences together extra special.

On October 13th, 1996, we were married. October of 2001 would have been our five—year anniversary. I could not believe how much we accomplished together in such a short time. When we were first married, we lived in a tiny one bedroom in Manhattan. In July of 2001, we moved into the house of our dreams that we had spent a year building together. We were both so happy upon moving to the suburbs. We were starting such a great chapter of our life together, and in such a short time, we made so many friends. You were so proud of our house, and loved to have people over to entertain.

You were motivated and hard working. You didn't ever mind getting on the six o'clock train each morning to commute to Manhattan. I know how much you loved your trading career at Cantor Fitzgerald. You started working with Cantor as a trainee on the trading desk, and within two years, you had become a partner. You developed such wonderful relationships with your clients. After September 11th, every single one of your clients called me with such concern and to express how much they missed you on a daily basis and that they truly enjoyed doing business with you. You were a friend to everyone, not just a typical businessman. I was so proud of you and how successful you had become.

The most important aspect of your life was becoming a father of our two beautiful boys. Ryan was almost three years old, and Ethan was nine months when you passed away. The boys loved you so much. When you would come home at night, their faces would just light up with joy. I remember how you couldn't wait to be home at night to spend time with them. Our house was always so noisy from all of the playing around. You were so proud of our kids, and talked about them all of the time. Any time that people came over, you would be so excited to show them all of their new endeavors. Our boys have the greatest personalities; they are so outgoing, happy and are always smiling just like you.

Marc, you were such a special person and had everything in the world going for you. You were good looking, smart, successful, easy going, and a wonderful family man. You were my best friend, and the best father that his children could ever have. You were the type of person who touched the lives of everyone who knew you. You were so warm, kind, and fun-loving, and a true friend to all. You were a person who really "loved life". You always had the most upbeat personality and positive outlook on life. While I cannot even begin to comprehend the way in which your life ended, I can celebrate the way in which you lived. Being that you were born on February 12, 1968, the same birthday as Abraham Lincoln, I always think about his famous quote: "In the end it's not the years in your life that count but the life in your years". I am so thankful that I was able to share the time that I did with you in our lives.

I still can't believe that September 11th happened 10 years ago. It still feels like yesterday. Since that day, I have been trying to perpetuate your memory by instilling your values in Ryan and Ethan and enjoying the kids to the best of my ability as you would have wanted to. The kids remind me so much of you, especially in the way they look and act. They are adorable, sweet and loving. They are so funny, always laughing and having a good time. They are also great athletes and love to play sports. They both play floor hockey and ice hockey like you did. Ryan loves to practice announcing the games and would love to follow in your footsteps and be a sportscaster at the University of Michigan. He follows all sports and knows every statistic from every sport. We still go to the Rangers hockey games with your father on a regular basis. Ethan loves the Rangers and is glued watching every game like you were. I sponsor an ice skating event every year to raise money for children's charities through the Marc S. Zeplin Foundation. The Foundation has allowed our family to turn a tragedy into a positive force. I am trying to live my life with the kids in a way in which you would have. I am so lucky to have such special children to constantly remind me of you. They help me to remember you each and every day and carry on your positive spirit in my life. That is what keeps me going every day. I will always love and miss you and will never stop thinking about you.

Love Always, Debra

Dear Marc,

My heart is heavy as I write these words. Even though it is close to ten years that you are not with us, we feel as if we lost you yesterday. The shock, the public nature of 9/11 and the reality that you and others just vanished without a trace does not enable many of us to realize closure. Each and every day is not the same without you, especially the ones that are supposed to be happy like birthdays, anniversaries and holidays.

However, even in passing, Marc, it appears that you still guide us. You have left behind a legacy of family, love and honor. Thoughts of you remind us to follow your example to live our lives with dignity and to focus on important matters, not the mundane. You leave us with so many memories of your humor, kindness and courage.

Since you truly are a man to remember, your family members decided to honor you in death as we did in life. Your loving wife Debra, your father Lenny, your sister Joslin, her husband Steven, your cousins Mitchell, Craig, his wife Debbie, and me are committed to the Marc Scott Zeplin Foundation which was immediately established to perpetuate your values.

You always demonstrated such a strong love for your children, Ryan, now 11, and Ethan, now 9, and had such compassion for disadvantaged kids that we decided that the mission of the Foundation would be to address the physical, social, emotional and educational needs of children of all races, creeds and religions.

In order to raise the revenue needed for our causes our Foundation holds fundraisers.

Your cousin Mitchell, with the support of Craig, has initiated and organized three amazing basketball tournaments at Chelsea Piers. In addition, Craig orchestrates an exciting rock concert in the Village each and every year featuring Tramps Like Us, a group who sounds similar to Springsteen, the man you so admired. Your multitalented wife Debra and a group of friends organize Family Fun Days in Westchester. A great deal of time and energy is spent in the planning and execution of the carnival and skating parties, but the end always justifies the means, especially when we see all the happy faces on the children who attend and realized the difference we could make in other children's lives with the proceeds. All of the Board members work hard to support the events and solicit donations and participation.

Initially, the Foundation provided financial assistance to organizations which supported children affected by 9/11. We later expanded our efforts by sponsoring events for children other than those affected by 9/11. For example, we paid for a Christmas party at the Ronald McDonald House where your father had the opportunity to dress up as Santa and distribute presents to all. We supported organizations that benefit autistic children and research centers seeking a cure for genetic diseases such as Disautonomia and Caravans.

We contributed to the Children's Hospital in Westchester to help implement a music program and to Friends of Green Chimneys, a school which meets the needs of emotionally, challenged youngsters. We provided funds to the Save the Children charity not only to alleviate the devastation caused by the tsunami but also to support educational programs in Bolivia and Uganda. We support the Westchester Pediatric Cancer Foundation and funded children in need as a result of the earthquake in Haiti.

We also provide college scholarships for deserving students. Most of the recipients have attended Oceanside High School. One of the most recent students calls you her special angel not only because of the funds she received to help with college expenses but because she was inspired by your deeds and zest for living.

More events are in the planning stage and we hope that the many people who have been so supportive will continue to be generous and involved.

Now while our actions and contributions sound like we are hardworking, generous and helping others, in actuality, we are really helping ourselves by displacing some of our grief into action.

In addition to the care and comfort provided by family and friends and the guidance given by therapists and support groups, to get through the tough times, we ascribe to the following formulas:

When the going gets tough, the tough get going.

When you least feel like it, you should try to do something for someone else.

It helps us to climb the hills and jump the bumps.

It gives us a purpose as opposed to only feeling sad and lonely for you . . .

We want you to know that memorials have been, and will be, specifically created for you and others in New York, Oceanside and Valhala, Westchester. Each year we return to that site where your sons have the opportunity to read your name and have often been televised doing so. However, for us, your children are the living testaments to the goodness we so violently lost on 9/11. Your son Ryan has special talents and intellectual gifts. He loves to read and is a walking encyclopedia of sports memorabilia. He has all the makings of a sportscaster, just as you did. Ethan displays your smile, mannerism and wit. He is a Rangers fan and loves to joke around and chatter just as you did. Both are excellent athletes. Debra ensures that they have ample opportunity to partake in all sports and even became a "hockey mom", a job she excels at.

We are all devoted to your family. We feel very close to Debra and have maintained the close connections we established from the onset. She considers our needs and always includes us in family activities, just as you did.

What an impression you made on so many! Four babies have been named in your honor. Your sister Joslin is married now and named her first born daughter Marielle Sloane; your dear friend Marla named her son Mason; and your cousin Mitchell remembered you as well when selecting a name for his son. In addition, Debra's sister and brother-in-law chose to name their third son Jordan Marc.

We all continue to listen to your songs, repeat your jokes and try to address obligations just as you would have shouldered them.

We will always keep your spirit alive and make you as proud of us as we were of you!

All my love,
Always,
Mom

Dear Marc,

It's been ten years since I've last seen or spoken to you, and the emptiness in my heart is still there. I miss you so much. Life is very different without you. You were always so much fun to be around and you always knew just the right thing to say.

There have been so many changes in my life that you were unable to share with me. Although your presence was always felt, something was missing from each event.

I married a man named Steven Paradise in 2006. I became a stepmother of his twin daughters, Eliza and Samantha. Shortly afterwards, we had a baby who we named after you—Marielle Sloane—and two and a half years later, a second daughter, Caroline Eve. As I write this letter to you, we are expecting our third daughter. I always tell Steven stories about you and we try to keep your spirit alive in our household. I think you would be great friends. When Marla met him, she said he reminded her of you because you have many similar traits. He went to Michigan and is close friends with your old friend, Marc Lewis.

You'd be really proud of your sons Ryan and Ethan. They are amazing athletes and are really well-rounded. Every time I look at them, I see a piece of you. Debra has been like a sister to me and we all spend a lot of time with one another.

I hope that wherever you are you are happy and at peace. You will never be forgotten and are remembered each and every day. I always feel fortunate that you were in my life and was always proud to call you my big brother.

Love,
Joslin

JAMES J. STRAINE JR.

James J. Straine Jr. was born on February 5, 1965 in Lawton, Oklahoma, to Jim and Mary Straine. He was the oldest brother to Michael, Katy, Kevin and Dan. Jimmy earned his BA from East Carolina University and after a short stint living in Charlotte, North Carolina, moved to Hoboken to work at Lehmann Brothers. After several years, he moved over to Cantor Fitzgerald. Jimmy married Tricia Carr in 1994 and they had two sons, Finn and Charlie (who was just 6 days old on September 11th). A Civil War buff, Jimmy also loved the East Carolina University Pirates football team, playing pick-up basketball, golf on the weekends with his buddies and relaxing at the beach. On September 11th, Jimmy was at his desk on the 104th floor of the North Tower. He was 36 years young.

Trish Staine-MacGregor (Wife)
Age: 42

Jimmy,

You were the love of my life, my best friend and a devoted father, son, brother, uncle, nephew and true friend.

Never before have I experienced a love as great as what you and I had. You gave me wonderful gifts—friendship, love, patience and understanding, but most of all, you gave me the privilege of being your wife and the mother of your children. On the first night I met you, I'll never forget noticing your big blue eyes, long eyelashes and shy sweet smile. You told me that night that you were going to marry me and we'd have ten girls that looked just like me. But it is I who struck gold that night and now have two beautiful boys who are just like their daddy. Finn and Charlie are so blessed to be the sons of such an amazing man—a true American hero and patriot.

When I think of you, so many images come to mind, but the one that stands out the most is of you walking home from work, down Washington Street, book in hand (usually something about the Civil War) and smiling as you saw Finn and I waiting for you on the corner. We loved to meet you and continue that walk-up to Kings or down to the pier or around the block to chat with the neighbors. You loved to talk—to anyone and everyone. When we first met, I would love to bring you to parties because I never had to worry about you—you always left a party with twenty new friends. You were the most interesting and well-read man I have ever met and you would crawl the walls if you didn't have a book to read. On September 10th, I convinced you to read the Harry Potter book that you gave me for Christmas last year.

You had so many interests—golf, fishing, ECU Pirates football, pickup basketball games, the Civil War, Ernest Hemingway, wildlife and a little known talent, lassoing lizards. You taught me how to chip and putt, how to spot an osprey resting in its nest atop a telephone poll, how to stop, look up and appreciate the stars in the sky.

Some favorite images that come to mind: eating a huge order of Triple Delight with Tabasco sauce all over it, riding your bike over to my apartment in Hoboken every single night to hang out, listening to an old REM CD, flying a kite over at the pier for Finn and checking out the fish just reeled in, grilling your rib-eye steak in the rain as you popped open another Corona, digging into your pint of Chunky Monkey while watching *Hannity & Colmes,* relaxing on the beach (any beach!) while listening to the FAN, searching for the latest college football magazine, walking through our front door soaking wet after a great game of basketball, planning the next Carolinas trip, rubbing my back and talking to my belly, rocking and kissing our baby boys, waking up at 5 a.m. to get a tee time, teaching Finn how to swing a golf club, catching Finn in your arms as he jumped into the pool, crying when I told you that I was pregnant with Charlie.

What will I miss? Your wonderful laugh, my goodbye kiss in the morning, finding Dunkin' Donuts coffee cups all over the floor of the car, the sound of the front door shutting as you walked in from work, watching you get dressed in the dark closet so you wouldn't wake me up, lottery tickets on the nightstand (the eternal optimist), the soft hair on your arms, your skinny legs and your beautiful soul.

You must know how blessed we have been by you, our angel.

I love you CP.

ANTONIO ROCHA

Antonio Augusto Rocha was born on February 8, 1967, the eldest son of Augusto Rocha and Rosa Rocha, in Paranhos da Beira, Portugal. At the age of four, Antonio immigrated to New York City with his parents where they later welcomed his brother, Jason Rocha. In May 1990, Antonio received a Bachelor's of Science in Finance with a minor in Economics from Manhattan College. On May 21, 1994 Antonio and Marilyn married. On March 2, 1998, Alyssa Marie Rocha was born. His son, Ethan Agustus Rocha was born on March 7, 2001. Antonio's hobbies were traveling, skiing, art, wine, golf, and mountain biking. He was employed at Cantor Fitzgerald as Vice-President of the Eurobonds Desk of Emerging Markets, Securities Department. On September 11, 2001, he was on the 105th Floor of the North Tower. Antonio was 34 years old.

Marilyn Rocha-Carmo (Wife)
Age: 39

Dear Tony,

There are so many things I want to say to you, that I don't know where to begin. I hope that you are at peace up in Heaven and that you know how much we miss you. The day my nightmare began, I was having a very normal day, as you know, getting Alyssa dressed for preschool and getting ready to feed Ethan his breakfast. I hadn't turned on the TV yet until you called me. I am thankful that you did because it was the last time I would hear your voice. I can still hear it, plain as day, in my head. I was sure my whole life had just fallen apart and I would never be able to recover again. You were my soul mate and the only boyfriend that I actually fell in love with. We were both so young, but I'm glad I had those years with you now. I want to remember you with that big smile on your face and that is the picture I always have in the back of my mind.

Fortunately, God is big, and with the help of support groups, therapists and family, I pulled myself together. I'm not going to lie to you, for a few months I was a complete mess as a person, and as a mother. I lost so much weight I looked unrecognizable and I wanted to drown my sorrows, so every time I was out with my sister or friends I would drink myself to the point of getting sick. I lost three months or maybe four of Ethan's baby days. I regret that so much. I also hate that you missed it as you were such a good Daddy. After all of the feeling sorry for myself, I managed to pull myself together and did begin to feel stronger; to believe that I could control my future and that I could raise these kids by myself. I knew it would be hard, but I was determined to do it and do it well, the way you would have wanted. I also found comfort in going to church and praying to God to give me strength, health and wisdom to carry on. I also found comfort in going to the cemetery where your body lay. Sometimes I would just sit in my car in front of your grave and talk to you. Did you hear me? I know you did, because you are my Guardian Angel now and I look to you to help me when I need it.

I ended up becoming very close with your childhood friend, after he came to visit shortly after your death. We were married in 2005 in Mexico. The kids were so excited, he gave rings to both of them and accepted them as his very own and became their adopted father. He has taken on the responsibility of helping me raise them and it has been very rewarding to have that family feeling back in our lives. Alyssa is now 13 and stands at 5'6", tall like you. She is such a beautiful girl and smart. She enjoys playing basketball, dancing, playing piano and texting on that new phone of hers. Ethan is 10, and also enjoys basketball, piano, guitar, taekwondo, football and baseball. He is a true boy; you would have had so much fun with him. He has so many expressions that remind me of you. He has such a big heart and is such a loveable little boy. They are both such great kids and I know that even though you can't be here, that you watch them every day.

I have accepted that you cannot be here with us, but I still don't have one day that goes by that I don't think of you for one reason or another. I hope that you are proud of me, for the way I have raised the kids and for the choices I have made. I am not perfect, but I try my very best to be a good role model for these two kids. The kind of love we shared only comes around once in a lifetime and that feeling is locked up in my heart in a very special place that only I can visit when I need to, and sometimes I visit it often. You changed my life and showed me things I thought I would never see. You taught me things, your love for me was shown through all the thoughtful things you did, not only on special occasions but just because, and that's one of the things I loved about you. You were so spontaneous and sometimes that made me crazy, but in the end, I loved that you were like that. It made life interesting and fun. Like the time you called me at work and asked if I wanted to go to Paris for three days. I thought you were kidding, but you weren't, and we had such a fun and romantic weekend.

When the kids were born, those quick getaways were over, but I loved watching you interact with them. You loved taking Alyssa to Disney World, and playing at the park with her. You would come home from work with stuffed animals for her, her eyes would get so big when you would come home holding one of them. I hope that her memory of you, even though it is small, will stay with her forever. Poor little Ethan has no memory of you except what I've told him and the pictures we have shown him. Remember the weekend we spent before that tragic Tuesday? We went to the Turtle Back Zoo and we rode on the train with both of them. I still have that picture of you and them on the train. That was the very last day we spent together as a family. We will keep your memory alive in Ethan, I promise you that.

I hope heaven is everything you could have imagined and that you can still see your beautiful kids from up above. We will never stop missing you or thinking of you. I hope I stick around long enough to see these kids well into their adult years, but when I have to go, I won't be afraid because I know you will come for me and make me feel safe. I will be joined with you again and that will be such a good feeling. I love you more than words can explain, and that will never change. I am getting teary just thinking of how much I love you and miss you. Please guide us in the right direction and be our Guardian Angel forever. We will look up to you for guidance and support and I know you will walk beside us when we need you.

Goodbye my beloved Tony, until we meet again.

Love always,
Marilyn Rocha (fofa)

FRANKLIN ALAN PERSHEP

Franklin Alan Pershep was born on March 30, 1942 in Manhattan, New York to Henry and Henny Pershep. He was big brother to Irene Pershep. Frank married Estelle Kupersmith in 1966 and they had two daughters, Sharyn and Stacy. Sharyn gave Frank his three grandchildren, Mackenzy, Heather and Hunter. Frank was Vice President of the Marine & Energy Division of AON Corp. He loved his family and loved spoiling his girls and especially his grandchildren. He was a well-known prankster both in and out of the office, and was often referred to as "The Bagel Man" since he brought Brooklyn Bagels to work on a weekly basis. On September 11, Frank was at his desk on the 98th floor of 2 World Trade Center. He was 59 years old.

Stacy Joy Pershep–Paolozzi (Daughter)
Age: 29

Dear Daddy,

It is hard to know where to start as so much has happened in the past ten years. We all have so much to tell you and I will try to include everything as best I can. I thought about making this letter silly and corny like you but I am not sure I can. We all still miss you so much, and besides I used to hate it when you got all goofy anyway!

A lot has changed in the past ten years and sometimes it feels like a lifetime ago when you were "missing", but mostly I still have to remind myself that you are gone. Every now and then someone will ask me a question like, "What is the best sushi spot in midtown?" or "How big of a suitcase can I bring on board an airplane?" and my immediate reaction is, "Let me call Daddy." I have a split-second moment when I think I can reach you and then I remember. It doesn't hurt as much as it used to, and now I mostly just laugh because I imagine you watching me and having a good giggle at my expense.

There is so much to tell you about the family but I want to be a little selfish and start with me. I know how worried you were about your single daughter. Well, I am not single anymore! In 2004, I met the most amazing man, Vincent. In my heart of hearts, I honestly believe that you were up there watching and orchestrating the whole thing. He is exactly what you wanted for me and everyone, even Aunt Irene and Tommy, think that you would LOVE him. He makes me happier than I ever thought possible. He takes care of me and spoils me just like you did. Many people have remarked on how much like you he is, and I can see it in some ways. From his job to his spending, from his passion for life to his sense of fun. Mommy loves him, too, and they have a great relationship. We got married on October 6, 2007, and it was a beautiful wedding, everything was perfect except, well, you weren't there. Sharyn was my matron of honor and pinned a picture of you to my gown and on my bouquet so

I could feel you with me. She really didn't need to, I knew you were there all night, especially when Mommy and I didn't fit down the aisle together or when Vin stepped on my train! I bet you had a good laugh!

Sharyn and Brian are still doing well and living in Bensonhurst. This June, they will be married 22 years. The kids, Daddy, you would be so proud. Mackenzy is in high school and doing great. Your miracle grandson is all grown up with a moustache (that we all try to get him to shave) and is mainstreamed in all his classes. You would never know he was a preemie! At 18, he is taller than me and almost as tall as his mom and dad. His Bar Mitzvah was a beautiful affair that would have made you proud. It was a food theme, as it seems your grandson wants to be a professional chef. Remember those wood projects you used to do with him? Well, he is taking shop in school and making the most amazing things. He just gave me a clock that is unbelievable! It looks like a store-bought mini grandfather clock but he made it. He misses you a lot and we talk about "what Pop would do" often.

Heather is a senior in junior high and giving Sharyn and Brian all the grief we gave you and Mommy when we were teenagers. She is going a little boy crazy already and still looks a lot like me! I still call her "mini me" and she, just like her brothers, still calls me Fava! I may never be Aunt Stacy. She is doing well in school and, like her Mom, she is loving her math classes. High school is next year and she is actually looking forward to it. No boyfriends yet, but her dad and Uncle Vin are all about intimidating the boys like you would have when they come knocking. She is a beautiful young lady so I am sure they will be coming around soon!

Hunter is in his first year at Mark Twain. He didn't want to go to at first but Sharyn and I talked him into it, pretty much the same way you talked us into it. He was accepted for Creative Writing like I was and actually has the same teacher I did. Although, he does do really well in math and science like Sharyn. It's a lot for him to get used to but he is doing very well and we are all super proud of him. I am sure he will have his pick of high schools when the time comes. He is such a cute kid and for some reason, reminds us all of you. It could be because he is a smart kid, or it could be because he is so stubborn.

Aunt Irene is still with Sy and doing well. Her breast cancer has not returned and she finally retired from the bank. She splits her time between her apartment in Manhattan and the one in New Jersey. If she is not there, you can find her on a cruise ship.

Mommy is still living in the same apartment and still struggling along. It was, of course, and remains, hardest on her. We all pitch in and try to take care of her the way you did, but boy, did you leave big shoes to fill. She is still going to Weight Watchers but we can't pay her by the pound the way you did. She is trying to get out there and do things, and recently has taken a few knitting classes. She began helping some of the other students with crocheting projects and now they want her to teach a class on crocheting at the library. She misses you very much, and tries to do the things for Sharyn, me and the kids that you would have done. It is not easy for her but each year that goes by she gets a bit stronger.

Last year, Vin and I bought an apartment in your favorite neighborhood, Park Slope! I can't believe I am a home owner. Sharyn is well on her way and is looking for the right apartment in Bay Ridge. I know you always wanted that for us. We are happy, and doing well. There is this big hole in all of our hearts that you left. We know we can't fill it, so we do our best to fill up all around it. When we lost you, we all discovered an inner strength that we never know we had. It was the most difficult thing I have ever gone through, and for each of us, it was a very dark time. I had to first learn to grieve *how* you died before I could grieve *that* you died. But we pulled together and leaned on each other and that helped. We do the things that you loved in your honor. I still go out for sushi every year on your birthday and feel you there with me urging me to eat the octopus or tip the sushi chef. Sharyn was president of the PTA and the "go to" chaperone for the all class trips, just like you and Mommy were.

When we sit and talk about you and tell all the funny stories, the things you did that made us so mad at the time, like calling me "fart breath" in front of all my friends in high school, we are smacked in the face with what an amazing father, husband, grandfather and brother that you were. We are thankful for the time that we had with you, the lessons you taught us, and all the times you made us laugh. My Daddy, the real life Peter Pan. We live our lives trying to make you proud and honor you as best we can. Losing you the way we did has made us discover who we are in a very different way. While none of us wants to let our loss define us, it has shaped who we are. I try to take comfort in knowing that you are a part of history now. We are so proud to see your name engraved in the memorials, or the street named in your honor. But it doesn't fill that hole, nothing will.

We miss you and we love you just as much today as we did ten years ago.

Love,
Half-pint
Stacy Joy Pershep—Paolozzi

JOSEPH A. LENIHAN

Joseph A. Lenihan was born on June 9th, 1960 in West Hartford, Connecticut, to Joseph and Ann Lenihan. Joseph was the youngest of six children: Mary, David, Sue, John and Betsy. Joe married Ingrid Cosentino in 1988, and they had three children, Megan, Gabriella, and Joseph. Joe received his BA and MBA from the University of Connecticut. He enjoyed his work for Keefe, Bruette & Wood, and had just become an Executive Vice President and Director of the Fixed Income Department. Joe loved his family, was involved in activities for veterans, in memory of his father, a WWII veteran; and Joe loved making everyone laugh. Joe was at his desk on the 89th floor of the South Tower, on September 11th. He was 41 years old.

Dave and Betsy Lenihan Smith (Brother-in-Law and Sister) Age: 55 and 55

Dear Joe,

The mention of your name immediately brings a smile to our faces. We automatically see your face smiling and the twinkle and kindness in your eyes.

You listened so intently to individual conversations, that at times, it was uncomfortable. It was the rare person who gave you their full and complete attention, as you did.

If someone was being untrue to themselves or others, you would spot this and call them on it, right away. You did not tolerate being unfair to others . . . or to oneself.

Therefore, when people spoke with you, they were true to themselves and to others. You didn't challenge their words, you just could see through to the truth, and gently helped us see it, too.

You may be able to imagine how much you are missed by our family, but we don't think it is possible. However, the thought of you still brings out our own innate ability to be the best we can be to ourselves and to humanity. You surely live on in all the people that you touched in your too short life.

Your dear friends started a collection soon after you died on September 11, 2001. We dedicated a memorial to you on the lawn of our high school, which included a tree, a bench and a large slab of marble remembrance.

We then began the process of seeking donations for scholarships in your name at Saint Thomas the Apostle, Hall High School and the University of Connecticut. Since 2004, a scholarship has been given in your name each year from the University of Connecticut. Ten needy students have been able to attend St. Thomas the Apostle Elementary School due to the scholarship.

They have a plaque in the main hallway listing those who have been awarded your scholarship. And fourteen Hall High students have been awarded money to help pay for college. Each year in your birthday month of June, we award these scholarships and know that you are smiling down on us. We believe you are with Dad in heaven and this helps Mom, who will be 87, and all of us go forward each day.

We, with our sister-in-law, Ingrid, and all the kids in our families, attempt to live each day the way we believe you would want us to. We gratefully thank all those people who helped us through one of the roughest times of our lives, we thank God and we thank you for the deepest gentlest manner in which you touched all our lives.

With so much love and gratitude for this book,

The Lenihans and all our very special extended families and friends

RONALD T. KERWIN

Lt. Ronald T. Kerwin was born on October 6, 1958, to William and Carol Kerwin. Ronny and his brothers, Kenny and Danny, grew up in Hicksville, New York. He married Dianne Pressler in 1985 and they have three children, Ryan, Keith and Colleen. Ronny started his career with the FDNY in September 1981 and was a Lieutenant in Squad 288, Maspeth, Queens. Ronny also joined the volunteer fire service in 1982 and was Chief of Department of the Levittown Fire Department in 2000 and 2001. He adored his family and enjoyed fishing and golf. On September 11th, Ronny and his company were evacuating the South Tower. He was 42 years old.

Maureen and Kevin Pressler (Sister-in-Law, Brother-in-Law)
Ages: 52 and 54

Dianne Kerwin (Wife)
Age: 51

Courtney Pressler Parver (Niece)
Age: 31

Dear Ronny

Just a note about a man, an Uncle, a Dad, a Brother-in-Law, a Hero, and a loving father to Ryan, Keith and Colleen. Ronnie, you know that your time on this earth gave us lots of pleasure and joy. I had the privilege of watching your daughter Colleen while your wife Dianne was at work and you were on your way home from the Fire Department in Masbeth, Queens. Watching and waiting at the door for her Dad was a gift all by itself. The joy I saw her experience when you arrived could warm your heart. Thank you for those times.

The times you spent with our children left many lasting impressions. Tim is a young man with lots of drive and focus which you shared. Matt saw your courage, your pride and selfless services to others and your willingness to help, which had a strong influence in his joining the Army. He hopes he can make a difference in the world as you have. John misses the fun at the beach house, the fishing and the family parties, which we shared with you. They were young but I believe they have learned what it is to give your all. The courage you have shown and your ability to lead has left a lasting impression on our boys.

Thank you and we love you.

Maureen and Kevin

Dear Ronny,

It's hard to believe that it has been ten years since that tragic day. The kids are "OK". As I believe you are watching over us, you know then that it's been a roller coaster ride.

I have tried hard to make life for the kids the best it can be. I guess at times I overcompensate because they no longer have a father. I made sure that I made every attempt to be at every game, match and show that the kids were in because I didn't want them to be the child with no parent watching them. As much as they would tell me it's OK if I can't make it, because it's difficult to be in two places at the time same, I always noticed how they would look up in the stands for me. Life at times was pretty overwhelming and I know the kids sensed the pressure I felt and my unhappiness. I feel very sad that I could not make a happier home for them. You were the one with the witty sense of humor and how I miss that laughter in our home. For a good part of those years, I was just trying to get through each day and that took everything I had. As I often say, I'm giving it the best I've got.

You have given us so many wonderful memories. The kids talk often about our yearly trips to Disney World. They realized that that first February without you we would not be going. It broke my heart when Keith asked me if we were ever going to go anywhere again. Even he knew how you planned our vacations and created so much fun for us. Yours are big shoes to fill!

I hope you know how much all those memories mean to us. We often talk about them. Ryan, Keith and I often remember how you liked to go for rides in the car. They still laugh when they remember asking you where we were going and you would say, "Crazy, we're going crazy! Want to come?" Then you'd take us somewhere by Robert Moses Beach to see the deer. They really laugh about the time that we were driving by the Jones Beach Tower, that I like to call "The Pencil", and you told them it was a rocket ship and we were going to the moon. You asked them if they packed their bag with clean clothes. You had them so convinced. They were so young that I don't know if Colleen was even born yet.

Colleen amazes me with the memories she has of you considering she was so young. She remembers "the dates" you had going to Mr. Tony's to get pizza for lunch. She loved that you told her she was your date. She also talks about how you would make her lunch before getting on the bus for kindergarten. You would ask her how she wanted her sandwich and she would sing to you the Backstreet Boys song, "I Want It That Way".

I'll never forget the one day only a few months after we were married that I came home from work and you asked me to guess what we were going to be doing over the February vacation. I remember telling you that we would be working on fixing up the house. You told me, "We're going to Jamaica". I thought you were out of your mind because we needed every penny we had to try to fix up the "handyman special" house we bought. I can remember as plain as day you telling me that we could die tomorrow and this mess of a house would still be here and how we had to take some time to live and enjoy ourselves. That's a lesson that I often have to remind myself of. Jamaica was one of many trips we took. You were the one to say, "Let's go". I miss the spontaneity you brought to our lives. Because of you, I have all those memories of Jamaica, Cancun, Bermuda, Florida, and New Orleans . . . Although I attempted to cancel the Disney Cruise that you had booked for us the July after 9-11, I was convinced into still going. Everyone felt that since it was your gift to us, as a thank you for the busy eight years you spent being a Chief with the volunteer fire department, when I had to take the kids. I did, but remember very little. It was a difficult trip. Thank goodness there were the Herolds, Brennans and Courtney to keep me going. I am also so thankful for all of those Julys that we had as a family together out east at our summer rental. I have continued those July beach house summers. Being out there has become my sanctuary.

I find that those first years without you are a blur. There is not much I remember. The kids will talk about something and say, "Remember when . . .", and I don't. Even now I find that I don't remember things of not that long ago. I get concerned that I'm losing my memory at an early age, but have been told (by professionals) that my brain is on overload. I am doing the job of two people and can only take in so much. It bothers me that before 9/11, I felt so together and felt like I accomplished things and felt productive. I feel like that part of me is gone. I miss the "me" I used to be. You were my partner, "coach" and my reassurance. With you I felt everything was, or would be, OK. I guess the best way to describe it is that I kind of feel like a kite without a string. I am not anchored and I am floating around—not sure of where I'm going. I just take one day at a time and to tell you the truth not much phases me anymore. I sometimes feel "numb" to certain things. I know it's not good, but I often think, "Expect the worst and anything you get is probably better than what you expected". I guess that's my way of convincing myself that if I think that way, then it won't hurt so badly or the disappointment won't be so bad. I really need to work on that. I worry the effect it will have on the kids. I used to be an optimist. I looked at the better side of things and focused on that. I was a pretty positive person. As I said before, I miss the old me. Maybe it's time to go back to counseling. Although, I recently met up with another wife (I hate the word "widow") and when she said something about how she tends to expect the worst so things won't seem so bad, I felt relieved. Seeing people who have "moved on" and seem to function much better than I, can get discouraging. I keep telling myself that people "move on" at different times and we're not all the same.

I truly know what you would want for me. After your friend, Kevin, died, I know how badly you felt for his wife and kids. I remember how glad you were when she started dating. I especially remember you walking on our front door and saying "Di, guess who's getting married?" You were so happy for her and I remember you saying that she should not have to spend the rest of her life alone. I know I need to "work on" that part of my life. Maybe I use the kids as an excuse, but my life was so busy with them that there was very little extra time.

I want you to know that even though there were some very difficult times these past years, I am so proud of our children and I know you would be, too. Ryan, who for years never mentioned the fire department, joined the volunteer fire department two years ago and recently transferred into your fire company. Keith is interested in construction. He built the beach stairs out east and has your "knack" for fixing and building. Colleen is passionate about horses. She rides a mare named Dixie almost every day. I only wish I knew more about your horse care/riding days from before I met you so I could tell her about it. Each of them has one of your major interests. It is comforting to see you living on in them, but at the same time it pains my heart that you're not here to share it with them. You could have shared so much with them and made such a difference in their lives.

I miss you more than words can say and love you with all my heart.

Love, Dianne

Dear Uncle Ronny,

It's been almost ten years since we last saw you and not a day goes by when I'm not thinking of what life would be like if you were still here. You would be so proud of your family. Your children strive to be the best that they can be with you shining down on them.

I remember when you and Aunt Dianne were dating and she was living at C.W. Post. She would babysit me and you would bring pizza for dinner. Even at the young age of two, I can still remember you walking through the door.

When Colleen was a newborn, I was over your house visiting and holding her while sitting on the couch. You and Aunt Dianne looked at me and said, "We want to ask you something. We would like you to be Colleen's godmother." With joyful tears in my eyes, I, of course, replied, "Yes!" I still remember us in the living room and still hear your voice to this day. That was one of the happiest days of my life. I hope that I am doing a good job being there for my cousin and your daughter.

On September 1, 2001, we were all at your house for Colleen's birthday party. It was just a couple weeks before that I had celebrated my 21st birthday. You and I had such a wonderful talk that day. I told you all about the celebration and how much fun my friends and I had. We talked about the fact that I was now of legal drinking age. I never got to tell you this, but I felt that our relationship had matured that day. The conversation was different. We spoke on more of a peer-to-peer level. I didn't feel like I was the kid and you were the adult. If that had to be my last memory, it sure is a good one to have.

We miss you so much. All the times out east, holidays, family get-togethers and vacations are missing your personality and humor. One day we will meet again. But in the meantime, please continue to watch over us and help us stay strong.

Love your niece,
Courtney

JOHN WILLIAM FARRELL

John William Farrell was born on January 23, 1960 in Brooklyn, New York, to Michael and Dolores Farrell. He had two brothers, Michael and Jim, and three sisters, Nancy, Kathleen and Maureen. He married his high school sweetheart, Maryanne Sullivan, 1984, and they have four children, Kaitlin, Patrick, Molly and Colin. John was managing director for Sandler O'Neill & Partners. He loved spending time at his beach house in Mantoloking, NJ with family and friends, taking naps and running on trails through Jockey Hollow Park. On September 11th, John was sitting at his trading desk on the 104th floor of the south tower. He was 41 years old.

Megan McDowell (Sister-in-Law on behalf of the Farrell and Sullivan Families)
Age: 41

Dear John,

It seems so strange to be writing you. I think all of us, all the people who love and knew you, have been writing you these types of letters in our minds for the past ten years. The words come to us when something happens and we turn to tell you about it or wait to hear you laughing or grab our arm to show us something the kids are doing. These types of letters have been thought about, not only when Kaitlin and Patrick graduated high school, or when Molly broke her ankle playing soccer, or when Colin wore #34 on his uniform jersey. I think we write these letters in our minds to you over the simplest of things: watching Maryanne put up the Christmas lights, Colin taking out the garbage or when we see your favorite type of butter sitting on the dinner table at the beach. We all talk to you, "write to you", in our own ways on a daily basis. Sometimes these "letters" are read aloud in the form of a memory or someone saying, "That is so John!" when Patrick falls asleep on the couch with a room full of cousins, aunts, uncles and siblings running past him, yelling upstairs and dropping potato chips on him as he snores. Sometimes we can talk about you without crying, sometimes we can't. (Nana always has to clear her throat).

There have been thousands of times when I can see on Maryanne's face that she is off somewhere with you in her mind's eye, not able to read her letter out loud at the moment, but certainly "writing" her thoughts to you. Your absence is difficult to explain. We see your name on the Walls of Remembrance, we hear it called on the anniversary each year from the podium where your building once stood, and there is always a spot on the sand where we want your beach chair to be. And yet, when we are all together, you *are* here—throwing the football, having a beer in your sunglasses and baseball hat. You are here in Molly's big blue eyes, at each of Colin's football games, at college with Kaitlin and Patrick when *Love Shack* is playing at a fraternity party. Your children are inexplicitly yours and we see it more and more as they become adults. Although your children were only 11, 9, 5 and 3 years old when you died, they are certainly your kids in the way they walk, talk and interact with people.

Curious things have occurred, like when Kaitlin was going to her first prom and the theme song from when you and Maryanne were crowned "King and Queen" in 1977 played on the radio an hour before the limo arrived. Your football #34 is consistently showing itself in Maryanne's checkbook, an address we need to get to, or an exit number just as one of us is feeling completely lost on a highway somewhere. Or Thanksgiving night of 2003 when Kaitlin played "Amazing Grace" on the bagpipes in your kitchen just before leaving for St. Joseph's Shrine to look at your name on the wall. While we stood there a few minutes later in the cold air, on the quietest of nights, the sounds of "Amazing Grace" began to play on the bagpipes somewhere off in the distance. We were in the middle of nowhere, and every single one of us heard it. We laughed and cried, knowing that you really are always with us.

What else can we write John, other than you were a great husband, incredible dad and loved by your family, extended family, friends and colleagues? You influenced so many people in your lifetime, and your death continues to have an effect on the entire world. We will love you in every way, every day for the rest of our lives.

Love,
The Farrell and Sullivan Families

DAVID ALAN JAMES RATHKEY

David Alan James Rathkey was born on April 28, 1954 in Maidenhead, England to Eileen and Colin Rathkey. He was the brother to Philip, Julia, and Angela. He married Julia Wilcox in 1984 and they have three children, Emma, Ian, and Matthew. David loved his family and especially loved playing, watching, and coaching soccer. David was a sales executive with IQ Financial on September 11th. He was 47.

Emma Rathkey (Daughter)
Age: 22

Dear Dad,

I always think about you this time of year, the New Year. I can't help but think about how I have another year ahead of me without you around. It's the little things we miss: walking in and seeing you reading a book and drinking a glass of red wine, watching *This Old House*, hearing you laugh, and listening for your car in the evening. These are things I took for granted as a child, as I never thought that my family could be hurt and broken apart. But it was, as so many other families were, and I had to learn to accept the most painful and horrible change that I had even been faced with.

I still remember that fateful day and waking up to hear you leave the house. I never got up to say goodbye. I remember thinking I will just try to go back to sleep, I will see you when you got back from work. If only I had known that you would never be returning home again. As the years have gone by, I have been able to live with my decisions and move forward. Especially with help from my 9/11 camp, America's Camp. After losing one of the most important people in my life, I was blessed with so many lifelong friends that I can trust wholeheartedly. These people mean so much to me and are there for me through thick and thin. My one wish is that they could have met you.

There is one line from America's Camp that was spoken by a staff member many years ago. He said, "If heaven is anything like this place, then they are doing just fine." I often remember this comment and realize that heaven is full of people from our past who love and care for one another. It is supposed to bring peace and happiness and release all other cares one may have. This is the exact same thing America's Camp has done for its campers. I have grown stronger and become more open to talking about you and the loss and pain that has come with it, from being a part of America's Camp. It has brought happiness and peace to everyone involved and for one week, released all our fears and worries. Even now that you and I are apart, I know we will never truly be apart because we share a sense of security and peace that has been given to us.

You loved soccer, or football as you fondly referred to it. You coached my team the entire time we had together: the Mountain Lakes Electrics. Every girl on the team seemed to enjoy practice and respected you. You always made it fun; you had one game that I know I hated. You would make us all line up in a single file line and you would stand at the front of the line with the soccer ball. It was a heading drill. We had to get up to a certain number before we could stop, and if we messed up, the count went back down to zero. Gosh, how I hated having to give a perfect header then race to the back of the line. Of course, as the coach's daughter, I was the first to complain, however nothing was ever done to change the game otherwise. I would try to argue that as the goalie I had no use for headers and that they gave me a headache. Your reply? "You are just doing them wrong." So with my tail between my legs, I would race into the line like everyone else. At least it was a game, right?

For the past ten years, there has been more change in my life than I had ever anticipated. None of which I regret, as I feel any experience has helped shape me into the person I am today. The most important thing I can say today is that you live inside of me each and every day. Not a day goes by without me thinking about you and remembering all you did for me and our family and how much you cared for us. As long as I can hold you in my memory and teach my future family of what a great man you truly were, your memory and the great life you lived will never be forgotten. And when I graduated from Connecticut College in the spring of 2011, you were right there beside me congratulating me for this major accomplishment in my life.

Thank you for remembering,

Emma Rathkey

TIMOTHY MATTHEW WELTY

Timothy Matthew Welty was born on February 27, 1967 in the Bronx, New York to Adele and Bill Welty. He was raised in Flushing, New York with his brothers Chris and Darren, and his sister, Melinda. Tim graduated from Archbishop Molloy High School, and attended Pace University and Long Island University, where he studied mechanical engineering. Tim married Delia Mastromauro on September 17, 1994 and they have two children, Jake and Julia Welty. Tim joined the FDNY in 1993 and was assigned first to Engine 233 in Brooklyn, then joined the Special Operations Command Unit Squad 288 in Maspeth, Queens. Tim enjoyed riding his motorcycle to work, skiing, sky diving and spending his time off with his family. He played ice hockey and volleyball for FDNY teams. He was the owner of Town & Country Builders, and was an experienced, talented carpenter and skilled auto mechanic. On September 11th, Tim raced to the Twin Towers on the back of the HazMat 1 Truck he wasn't assigned to that day. His body was recovered on December 11th in the rubble of the North Tower along with two of his fellow firefighters. He was 33 years old and in the prime of his life. He is very deeply and sorely missed.

Julia Welty (Daughter)
Age: 9

Dear Dad,

You are my hero. You were a New York City Firefighter in Squad 288 in Queens, New York. You died in the 9/11 tragedy. You and 18 other men in your firehouse raced to the World Trade Center to try to save lives and property. This is what they did every day. You risked your life for more than 25,000 people, and you helped save most everybody in the Twin Towers. You were very strong and brave, and I've always looked up to you. That is why you are my hero!

Your qualities are very inspiring. You were helpful because you had saved MANY people from fires. You had saved peoples' houses and businesses. You were protective because you protected the things that people own. You were brave because you risked your life for other people all of the time, day and night, in small houses and tall buildings. You were well-trained because you knew how to dress yourself properly when going into fires and what equipment to use. Lastly, you were very clever. Once you used your hand to spray water on an apartment fire from a hose that lost its nozzle! These qualities and many others are what make you my hero.

You had brown hair, brown eyes and a round nose. You were very tall, 5 feet 11 inches. You were very fit and strong, and had broad shoulders. You had a HUGE smile and white teeth. You were agile and very athletic. You played baseball, volleyball and ice hockey. You were a real daredevil when you were growing up. You used to jump off the garage roof and climb up trees. You broke almost all of your fingers when you were growing up. You weren't afraid to do anything. As an adult, you were a downhill skier, a skydiver and a motorcycle rider. You were a great carpenter and built many things like roofs, stairs, patios, beds, chairs, tables, floors and fireplace mantles. You even renovated Granny's whole house! Lastly, you were very careful and smart around fires. You were a great dude and I'm proud of you.

I admire you because you were never thinking about yourself when you went to the World Trade Center that day. You were only super excited to accomplish the hardest thing in the world: a terrorist attack on the United States, in New York City. Saving 25,000 people was the greatest rescue mission in the history of the United States. You did this work every day you went to the firehouse. It didn't matter what kind of people were in a fire, you tried to save them anyway. You had great passion for what you did. You loved being a firefighter.

You are a bigger hero than any other hero because you died trying to save 25,000 people, and they were complete strangers. You didn't have to go there that day, but you did because you loved your job. You were very committed to your job. In my opinion, you were awesome and great! You are the biggest HERO of all!!!!!!!!

Love,
Julia

PETER MOUTOS

Peter C. Moutos was born on February 2, 1957 in Amarillo, Texas to Gus and Gladys Moutos, the brother of Linda and step son of Lannette. Peter married Meg Cooney in 2000. He earned a degree in business administration and worked for Marsh & McLennon. Peter loved his family and friends. He enjoyed working out and staying fit. On September 11th, Peter was at his desk on the 100th floor of the North Tower. He was 44 years old.

Meg Belding (Wife)
Age: 52

Dear Peter,

We met on a sailboat through mutual friends, and you took my phone number after the event; at that time, I never expected to hear from you. You were going to go to another social gathering with the "gang" from the boat. I, being a nurse, had work the next day so I needed to be home by a decent hour.

To my surprise, I heard from you that very same week. You tried to book me for the next weekend but I was already booked for a date. You asked me with persistence for a date the following weekend but I was working. You finally asked, "Well, when are you available?" I said, "In about three weeks." You said, "In that case, I am going to set up two dates with you!"

By the third date, I felt like I had known you all my life. We had such fun exploring Manhattan together. You, having lived in the City for 10 years, knew it so well. We enjoyed shows and museums together, jogging through Central Park, and going to great little restaurants that you had come to know over the years.

As I look back on my life, this was one of the most joyous times. We took time getting to know one another. Since I had recently moved to Long Island from Boston and your family was in Texas and California, we were "joined at the hip." We did everything together and became true soul mates.

After 9/11, I realized I had to recreate my future. I can honestly say that if it wasn't for so many caring people that were so kind towards me, I would not be as far along as I am today.

People sent me memorial tapes and books of you. Many people confirmed what I had experienced on a personal level. The consistent memories were your diligence as a worker, your sense of humor, and your generous spirit. You always were a team player and helped a colleague in need. Your friends and co-workers helped keep your memories alive for me, which were so needed.

The local community was supportive, too. The local dress shop saw that I was admiring an item in their shop and they knew I was a 9/11 widow. They asked me if I liked the item and then just said, "It's on the house," and gave it to me! The local framing shop did something similar. I had a life-size photo being re-glassed for your funeral and they did it at no charge and finally the local funeral home did all their service gratis.

Their acts of kindness were like a healing balm over a gaping wound. It helped clean away the wound of mourning and loss and helped me believe that life was still beautiful.

My friends were a great support; they encouraged me to move on. The closest friends to you would say, "You know, Peter, would want you to move on and live a happy life." At the time, I was continuing my education to become a certified school nurse. With their encouragement, I continued with my education and I am now a nurse for a special needs school.

I have since remarried to a wonderful man whom I met while ballroom dancing. Also, I have two wonderful accepting step-children. Today, I have a full life: more than I could have ever dreamed or hoped for.

I miss my soul mate. However, I would not ever give up the opportunity to have met you and fallen in love with you even if I knew such a tragedy was going to happen.

You added so much joy to my life that I will always carry the love you gave me in my heart and share it with as many people as I can.

Also, being a recipient of a community that cares, I realize how much the kindness of others can change a life. My hope is that whether at work or at play that I may return the great gifts of kindnesses that in so many ways have been shown to me.

Miss you and love you.

Meg

DEREK STATKEVICUS

Derek James Statkevicus was born on May 26, 1971, in Endicott, New York, to Joseph and Nancy Statkevicus, brother of Joel. Derek earned his BS in Accounting from Ithaca College and worked as a Research Analyst for Keefe, Bruyette & Woods. Derek married Kimberly Young in 1998 and they had two children together, Tyler (in August 2000) and Derek "Chase" (born in January 2002). Chase never had a chance to meet his father. Derek loved his family, his dog Squirt, and the New York Yankees. On September 11th, Derek was at his desk on the 89th floor of the South Tower. He was 30 years old.

Tyler Statkevicus (Son)
Age: 11

Kimberly Statkevicus (Wife)
Age: 40

Dear Daddy Derek,

There's a hole in my life without you. I miss you Daddy.

Love,
Tyler

Dear Derek,

I can't believe it has been ten years since your death. So much has happened in those ten years, yet at times it seems like just yesterday we returned from the Outer Banks and were planning our trip for summer 2002 with two boys instead of one. But then September 11th happened and shattered those dreams. It was such a horrific day and I can't imagine what you went through; I pray that you didn't suffer. The boys and I haven't forgotten you at all and we think about you daily.

Although you never got to meet your namesake, Derek "Chase", I have made you real for both him and Tyler. We talk about things you liked to do, tell funny stories about times we had together, and look at pictures and videos of our life together before you died. Every summer, the boys spend time with your parents and we see your brother frequently as well. We visit where we used to live and hang out annually, so the kids learn about our old life together. We all miss you!

Both boys are handsome, super-smart and energetic. They love dogs so much that now we have two. Tyler and Chase are both active in scouting and it looks like they are headed on the path to Eagle Scout someday, just like you. You would be so proud of them! Life at home can be chaotic, but it is a stable household full of love, despite what we have endured. The boys are so much fun and are thriving!

Tyler is your spitting image. It is uncanny but he looks just like you in every way. He even has expressions that you once made, proving, surprisingly, that it is nature rather than nurture. He's no longer the one year-old whom you fed birthday cake to. He is in middle school now, taking greater responsibility, and being more insightful. Chase physically resembles me more, but often he will do something that channels you, too, and it makes me smile. He wants to be an architect, just like you once wanted to be. He is generous, a hard worker, and quick to give a loving hug.

As for me, your death changed my outlook on life and I appreciate the person I have become. The expression "don't sweat the small stuff" is my new mantra. I'm sorry for a lot of the petty disagreements we had. While the issues may have seemed so important at the time, in the big picture many of them weren't. (Not all, but many!) I recognize that life is too short to hold grudges and the most important 'things' in life are really people—family and friends. You would not believe how people rallied around our family in our time of need. I couldn't have done it without them. I let down my walls and accepted help when I needed it most. It was humbling and liberating and it was the greatest gift ever.

One would think that after suffering such a great loss we might be spared for life, but that's not how it works; unfortunately there are no guarantees. Besides your death, our family has been dealt various other challenges over the years, but we've weathered these storms, too. Once you've survived hell, you know you are capable of getting through anything and all else becomes easier to deal with.

I never thought I'd be able to carry on and do it all without you, but God has provided, giving me strength I didn't think I had. I've often turned to the Bible and found Romans 8:28 particularly encouraging: "And we know that in all things God works for the good of those who love him, who have been called according to his purpose." (NIV) The past ten years have not been easy but the boys and I have had so many unbelievable blessings bestowed on us, too. Despite the tragedy, our life is good. We are fortunate and I am grateful. We stay centered on God and the life He has given us. The boys and I live our lives the best we can, in honor of you, because your life was taken too soon. We love you, Derek! Someday we'll see you again in heaven . . .

Love,
Kimberly

STEVEN PATERSON

Steve Bennett Paterson was born on January 21, 1961 in Hazlet, New Jersey, to George and Kathryn Paterson, the brother of George, Joseph, and Lois. On June 11th, 1995, Steven married Lisa Bornemann, and together they have twins, Lucy and Wyatt. Steven attended Raritan High School in Hazlet, New Jersey, and fresh out of high school, headed to Wall Street until the day he died. He cherished being with his family more than anything, and loved playing all different sports with his children. Steven was such a caring, wonderful, fun father to his children, adored his wife Lisa and enjoyed his friends and family. On September 11th, Steven worked at Cantor Fitzgerald, on the 105th floor of the North Tower. He was 40 years old.

Lucy Paterson (Daughter)
Age: 14

Wyatt (Son)
Age: 14

Dear Dad,

I can't believe it has already been ten years since you have been gone. Everyone misses you so much and wish you could be with us.

A lot has happened over the years and now Wyatt, Mom and I have grown. Mom has been incredible—I really can't even give a word to describe it. She has been amazing for us. After you died, she had to become the mother AND the father, and she's doing a remarkable job of it. She really likes playwriting now and being at the beach. Wyatt is such an incredible baseball player and snowboarder, and his personality always shines (even with his disability). You would be so proud of him. You would finally be having that conversation with him that you wanted.

I'm in my last year of middle school now (I know, can you believe it?). I'm doing tennis, lacrosse, and snowboarding and I really love it. I wish you could cheer me on and just be here when I need to talk and laugh. Wyatt and I always wish you could be here seeing how much we have grown and how much we have accomplished. These past ten years though have had their extreme ups and downs, but you know that our family is strong and we can battle through anything! We do know you are watching over us, and hope you are so proud of all we have done. We miss you so much Daddy, and we love you.

Love you always,
Lucy and Wyatt

JOHN RODAK

John Michael Rodak was born on September 29th, 1961 in Wilkes Barre, Pennsylvania, to John and Regina Rodak. He married Joyce Kenish Rodak and they have two children, Chelsea Nicole and Devon Marie. John earned his Bachelor of Science degree in Business Administration from LaSalle University and worked for Sandler O'Neill and Partners. He loved his family and partook in many hobbies, including his favorite, fishing during the summers in Ocean City, New Jersey. On September 11th, John was working in his office on the 104th floor of the South Tower. He was 39 years old.

Chelsea Rodak (Daughter)
Age: 20

Jared Kenish (Nephew)
Age: 23

Dear Dad,

I cannot believe it has been ten years since you have been gone.
A lot of things have changed.

When you left, I was just starting fifth grade. Now I'm in college
and I am studying sign language interpreting. Remember, I was
supposed to be a teacher? It is so different now. Devon is in high
school and I've had my license for a couple of years now.

Everything has changed. I miss you so much.

I remember your laugh and smile.
I remember how you would dance to the song *Hey, Must Be The
Money* by Nellie.
I remember how you would talk like Kermit the Frog all the time.
I remember when you said, "Good night, sleep tight, don't let
the bed bugs bite," every night before we went to bed.
I remember how you would let me stand on your hands and
you would lift me up and let me grab your feet. I always felt like
I was flying.

You are my best friend and I cannot believe you are gone. I remember that day when I found out that you were never coming home again. I always just used to say that you were on a long business trip or that you have amnesia and you just are walking around not knowing who you are and where you are from. Sometimes theories are better than reality. My theories were wrong. Part of me still wants to believe that you are out there somewhere but my heart knows that you are not. Sometimes I want to wake up and have it all be a bad dream and I will go downstairs and see you watching TV with your sushi and martini. This bad dream has been going on for ten years and I cannot wake up from it. Trust me, Dad, I've been trying. Every day and every night, I have been trying to wake up and so has everyone else in our family. Mom had been so strong for both of us. You would have been so proud of her. Devon is doing well in school. You need to see the mature young woman she is becoming. She is definitely not the little five year-old girl you remember and I am not the little ten year-old girl you remember. I am 20 years old now.

We miss you so much, Daddy. We will see you soon. I love you.

Love,
Chelsea

Dear Uncle J.R.,

I can't believe that it has been ten years since the last time we've seen you. It feels like just yesterday that all of us (the family) were down at the Shore having a great time sitting on the beach, walking on the boardwalk, and enjoying each other's company. It never really seems to get any easier as the years pass. When a loved one passes on, you expect to mourn their loss and then move forward by only remembering the good times. But in this situation, that dreadful day is relived every September 11th by all of us here who love and miss you with every ounce of our being. It's almost like on this one day out of the entire year, time stops and rewinds, causing us to feel exactly what we were feeling on that sunny, yet dark, Tuesday morning in 2001. But I refuse to let these awful events take away what I do have: the wonderful memories of you that I hold in my heart.

The memories that bring me the most joy are those from our family trips down to the Jersey Shore. As far back as I can remember, we made weekly weekend trips down to Ocean City in order to enjoy our time off from work or school, and relax away in the luxuries of the sun, sand, and surf. The thing I enjoyed the most were our fishing trips out on the bay. You would always wake me up at around 6:00 A.M., and we would go to the bait and tackle shop, and then head down to the All-Seasons Marina where the boat would gently rock in its dock waiting for us to arrive. So many a Saturday morning, we would do the ritual and then sit out on the gentle bay for hours at a time hoping to catch some flounder to bring home and cook for the family. Our trips would be so much more enjoyable when Devon, Chelsea, and Brandon would join in on the fun, giggling as we would speed through the waves to catch some wind.

I remember the last time we were all on board as a family. We weren't going fishing, but everyone was there for a nice trip out on the bay before the summer was over. Aunts, uncles, cousins, sons, and daughters were all there for a final hoorah before school was about to commence for another year. Unfortunately, that was the summer of 2001, some of the last memories we would have of you. Even so, they remain close to my heart and I know that they remain close in the heart of all of us here who love you so much.

There are so many moments in my life where I just wish I could bring you back. Knowing that there isn't any way around it still pains me. However, I know that you wouldn't want your loss to stop my life. I haven't let it nor will I ever.

After an intense four years of high school, I went on to college to get my Bachelor's Degree in Theatre Arts. I am now working on my Master of Arts in Theatre Studies and hope that next year I can go on for my Ph.D. My heart and soul is in teaching and theatre. I want to be able to inspire others to be serious about the things that they love. I also have another aspiration. I hope that one day I can open a non-profit performing arts organization that would help children and teens who have experienced a traumatic experience and show them that there is hope and that there are productive ways to release these experiences without self-destruction. After that dreadful day, I turned to theatre. Besides our amazing family that we have here, theatre was my saving grace and I want to be able to share that with others.

I hope that everything is going alright up there in the sky. I can just picture you, Grandpop and Grandmom Kenish playing a game of Pinochle, having a martini, and enjoying yourselves. Although we miss you down here, it is comforting to know that all of you are in good company. It's also very comforting to know that you're looking down on us in all of our endeavors, helping to guide the way.

One day we shall all be reunited, but until then, throw that boat into full throttle and enjoy the beautiful view from up above.

Love your First Mate and Nephew, Jared

JAMES MUNHALL

James D. Munhall was born on July 12, 1956 at Astoria General Hospital in Queens, New York to Donald and Marie Munhall. He was the brother of three sisters, Maureen, Kathleen and Patricia. Jim earned a bachelor's degree from St. John's University in 1978. He married Susan Ann King on June 8, 1991 and they had one daughter, Lauren Elizabeth Munhall. Jim joined Sandler O'Neill and Partners in 1993, where he was a Managing Director. Jim loved his family, riding bikes with his daughter and he loved watching his favorite team, "The Yankees". He enjoyed sitting with Lauren and teaching her the baseball stats. Jim was on the 104th floor of 2 World Trade Center on September 11th, 2001. He was 45 years old.

Marie Munhall (Mother)
Age: 83

Susan King Munhall (Wife)
Age: 48

My Dearest Jim:

Where do I begin? How do I compile 45 wonderful years into a few short pages?

Dad and I had two beautiful little girls—ages 3 and 6. Then on July 12, 1956, God sent us a baby boy. I know God went to this special garden and chose the cream of the crop to send to us.

It was a little difficult to explain to your sisters, Maureen and Kathleen, that your name was James, but we could call you Jimmy. Hence, when friends asked your sisters what your name was, they replied "Jimmy James". To this day, Jim, when we wanted to show a term of endearment, we all called you "Jimmy James".

Typical of sons, I had to be in your view at all times. Remember our laughs when I would say "Jim, look at my hips—one is higher than the other?" That's because I had you on my hip practically till you started dating. A little exaggeration, ha, ha. There are a million of these small memories that only have meaning to us.

God was good to our family—I just wish we all had more time together.

Your little sister, Patricia, arrived as a 7th birthday gift to you on July 9, 1963. You taught her to become the neighborhood Tom Boy. There was never time in her life for dolls or tea sets. Her big brother always had an extra football helmet and football or a baseball and bat for her. And, when you have a hero, isn't it normal to emulate him? Make no mistake, you were a hero to all three of your sisters.

You had your first job at 5 ½ years of age. The husband and wife across the street worked and since we lived on a dead end street, you would cross over to retrieve their garbage cans that were blowing all over. Another neighbor told them the little boy across the street was bringing in their cans. Immediately, the lady put you on her payroll at 25 cents a week. From time to time you would receive a nickel or a dime raise, and also a nice Christmas gift.

You eventually moved on to greater endeavors. As soon as you turned 12, you became eligible for a paper route. Many of your customers hired you to mow their lawns and shovel their snow-covered driveways. You were never one to pass up a job.

After graduation you enrolled at St. John's University. On your first day you met a wonderful friend, Mark Rosen. The friendship was sealed for life. After a few years, Mark asked his parents if you could move in, as he felt the drive from Commack was too much for you. The Rosen family welcomed you with open arms and Mrs. Rosen called you her, "Bubbala".

After graduation (Mark first, then you) you both found your true loves, Patty and Susan. You were best men for each other. Eventually, you joined Mark at Sandler O'Neill where Mark was your supervisor. You continued your wonderful friendship sharing triumphs and setbacks.

You and Susan were married June 8, 1991. What a wonderful day this was. Your marriage was based on mutual love and consideration. I think you know that Susan was your guardian angel through two bouts with cancer. Thank God you were cancer-free when tragedy struck on 9/11.

We were all blessed with a silver lining when Lauren Elizabeth was born on September 30, 1994. What a nice surprise for you and Susan. You were so grateful and thankful to be blessed with this beautiful baby girl.

Lauren and her Dad designated Saturday as their day to be best pals and do everything together. You added a new day to the week: Saturday became "Dadurday". Starting with a trip to the coffee shop for cocoa and cookies, you planned your day—T-ball, bike riding, etc. and you packed more quality time into your seven short years than some people enjoy in a lifetime.

If you were still here, Jim, I would hear you say one of your favorite quotes, "I'm so proud of you, Susan. You are doing an outstanding job raising our daughter. She is beautiful, respectful, and a delight to everyone who has the pleasure to meet her."

Yes, Susan has dedicated her whole life to her. She is involved with her sports. They often travel many miles for her lacrosse and other teams. Lauren didn't have too many years with her dad but her mom has taken over the job of two parents.

Jim, you were always a pleasure to our family. I'm sure Dad and your big sister, Maureen, have welcomed you with open arms. God bless all three of you in his care.

I still hear from some of your boyhood friends. It is so uplifting when they reveal how highly they think of you. One person reminds me often of how you helped him. He said for a while his life was off-kilter. You helped to straighten him out. For that he is most grateful and prays every day for you.

Jim, our last conversation on 9/11/01 was the following:

"Bye, mom, I love you."

I replied, "Bye, Jim, bye and God bless you."

Love,
Mom and family

Dear Jim,

You are my sunshine, my only sunshine.

I am a better person for having known and loved you. Thank you for the love, laughter and happiness that we shared. What we had was beyond what I ever could have imagined.

I will love you and miss you all the days of my life.

Susan

JOHN ANTHONY CANDELA

John Anthony Candela was born on February 23, 1959 in East Orange, New Jersey to John and Phyllis Candela, brother of Valerie, Karen Ann, Joan and Joseph. John married Elizabeth Davis in 1990 and they have two children, Juliette and John. John earned his Associate's degree from Morris County College. After college, he worked for Shearson Lehman for 13 years before joining Cantor Fitzgerald as a Senior Trader. John's happiness came from the loves of his life: Beth, Juliette and John. He enjoyed his Mustang, his music and his passion for playing guitar. John was a very giving and loving person, and touched many lives. On September 11, 2001 John was on the 104th floor of the North Tower. He was 42 years old.

Phyllis Candela (Mother)
Age: 79

Dear Johnny,

I am missing you.

I just love you and I miss my Kook-a-Luke. You always wanted to make people laugh. Johnny, you were my "funny man". You always made Mommy laugh. I love you more and more each day.

Johnny, Daddy was lost without you and he could not stand the pain of missing you. So, God took him with a massive heart attack five months after you were murdered. When Dad died, he had a smile on his face because he knew he was going to see you again. I can't tell you how much Daddy loved you and proud to say "my son" and I know for sure that Joey misses you, his "big brother"; and your sisters miss you too. We all miss you.

I want you to know how very proud I am of my grandchildren, they respect me as their Grandma. Beth is doing a great job. She continues to call me Mom and that makes me happy and proud that you married a woman like her.

I know Daddy came to join you and I am sure that he is in Heaven with you; and you also got to meet your sister, the first Karen.

When God says it's time for me to come, I will be happy to see you.

Keep taking care of the family, Johnny. We love you.

Here is a poem Dad read shortly after you were taken from us. It reminded him of you.

at the rising of the sun and at its going down . . .
at the blowing of the wind and in the chill of winter . . .
at the opening of the buds and in the rebirth of spring . . .
at the blueness of the skies and in the warmth of summer . . .
at the rustling of the leaves and in the beauty of autumn . . .
at the beginning of the year and when it ends . . .
as long as we live, he too will live, for he is now a part of us . . .
when we are weary and in need of strength . . .
when we are lost and sick of heart . . .
when we have joy we crave to share . . .
when we have decisions that are difficult to make . . .
when we have achievements that are based on his . . .
as long as we live, he too will live;
for he is now a part of us . . .
We will remember him

I love you Johnny, always have, and always will.

Mom

ANNMARIE RICCOBONI

AnnMarie Davi Riccoboni was born on September 11, 1943 in Astoria, New York, to Frank and Mary Davi. AnnMarie married John Riccoboni on November 14, 1965, and she was a wonderful mother to Maria-Elena and Janine. On that bright sunny day, September 11th, 2001, AnnMarie's 58th birthday, she was on her way to work for Ohrenstein and Brown and never returned home. She was 58 years old.

Maria-Elena Santorelli (Daughter)
Age: 45

Janine Passelis (Daughter)
Age: 40

Mom,

We cannot believe you were born on September 11 and that was the day you were taken from us. The youngest of six children, you enjoyed growing up in an adult world of this large family and began shaping your family values at an early age.

In May 1957, Grandpa, your dad, was the victim of a senseless killing. You went from being Daddy's little girl to a grown-up almost overnight. At thirteen years old you took on many responsibilities of an adult. You did this with all your heart and with no complaints.

We are told you were well-liked and respected by your peers and teachers. You were always busy with school, church, family and friends. But never too busy to lend a hand to someone who needed help, or to sit and listen to a friend with a problem, or to be there for Grandma, who was battling cancer.

It was after high school, that you and Felicia became close friends. You formed a wonderful friendship built on respect, trust and love. You had such good times and many, many laughs. She says you had a wonderful sense of humor, and you were the first to laugh at yourself if the occasion arose. Felicia always said you loved life and everyone who was a part of it. But above all, you loved God.

Being a truly spiritual person who had a special relationship with God, it was no surprise when in 1962 you told your friends and family that you thought you had a vocation and wanted to be a nun. This decision didn't go over too well with a lot of people, they were selfish and wanted to keep you there as part of their lives.

With a few trips to Long Island and Upstate New York, your friend Rosemarie drove you to a few different convents for interviews and meetings with the Mother Superiors of different orders. Your friends thought they would snatch you up, but the rejections came and the reasons had nothing to do with your spiritual side. One read, "considering the state of your mother's health and your being the only child who still lives at home, we cannot accept you at this time."

Although you were disappointed with their decisions, you accepted them as God's will and prayed for direction to get on with your life. And this seemed to set the precedent for the way you handled all your decisions in your life . . . bring everything to the Lord, pray, listen and accept His decision.

So the next few years you and Grandma were closer than ever. You took care of her, as she started losing her battle with cancer, and you were always happy and sometimes irritatingly cheerful.

In 1964, you were engaged to Daddy. November 14, 1965 you became Mr.and Mrs. John Riccoboni and you began your married life together.

The following August 1966, you gave birth to your first daughter, Maria-Elena. We are told you were thrilled during your entire pregnancy and ecstatic upon giving birth. You were totally devoted to your new little girl and just couldn't get enough. And so the next few years were good ones.

But in the spring of 1969, Grandma became very ill and, for the first time, you couldn't help her. You had been ordered bed rest, due to a difficult pregnancy, and were unable to be with her during her final days on earth. It was a sad time for you, not only did you lose your mother, but you also lost the baby you were carrying. You took time to mourn both but in your typical way, you came through it all stronger than ever. Never for a minute did you doubt that God was in control.

And in control He was, because the following September 1970, your second daughter, Janine was born. So now you had another little girl to dote on and love. And dote you did. We knew from little girls that we could always turn to you for safety, whenever we needed protection, reassurance and love. You loved your family unconditionally.

The next years seemed to fly by. You were always on the run and even though you now held a full time job, you were still always there for us. During these years you lost both of your sisters, Vivi and Lilly, and your two brothers, Sal and Jimmy, to cancer. It was not an easy time but again you walked in faith and accepted it all.

You were even upbeat in 1989, when you were diagnosed with a large growth on your thyroid. Surgery was necessary in determining malignancy. And, of course, you prayed and trusted in the Lord. Relieved to hear after surgery that you were cancer free and that the thyroid was removed and the large growth was nowhere to be found! It had disappeared! Were you surprised? NO! Were you delighted? ABSOLUTELY! You had left everything in God's hands and were prepared for any outcome.

The year 1991, found you and Daddy helping plan my wedding to my finance, Ralph. You were very happy with my choice for a husband and anxious to add a new son to our family. You were a great mother-in-law. You and Ralph shared private jokes and could be heard teasing one another. But you really had lots of respect for each other.

Then came the day you found out you were going to be a grandmother. You were so happy and full of joy. Your constant prayer was for a healthy pregnancy. July 1994 you all hurried out to the hospital in Long Island in time to greet your first and only granddaughter, Victoria Ann. You never missed the opportunity to flash pictures. A few years later, you were just as excited on the anticipated arrival of your first grandson and you had everyone you knew praying for a safe delivery, since I was having some complication with the pregnancy. You were there for the birth of Anthony Alfredo. Anthony will always remember having breakfast with you, the morning of September 11, 2001, your 58th birthday, as you prepared him for his day at nursery school. You were so proud of me. You marveled at my ability to do it all . . . be a good wife, mother, hold a job and take care of a home. But they say, like mother, like daughter. We are so glad we had your birthday celebration with Daddy, Janine, Ralph and your grandchildren just two days before you died. This was the last picture taken of all of you together. The look on your face says it all. You were so happy and content when with us.

In the spring of 1999, you were diagnosed with breast cancer and had decided, after much prayer and deliberation, to have a radical mastectomy. You asked God to be with you through this difficult surgery. You were never intimidated by the thought of dying. You always said you were prepared for heaven should you be called there suddenly. You had a strong feeling you would be the person in your family who would beat this horrible disease.

And beat it you did. After surgery you were pronounced cancer free. You were a true SURVIVOR! In May of 2001, you celebrated your first year as a survivor by walking with us, your daughters, Maria-Elena and Janine, in the Revlon Breast Cancer Walk. We remember what a special day we had with "*our mom*". We laughed, cried and just marveled in the wonderful day it turned out to be and we were so proud of you.

Early 2001, you found yourself busy helping your daughter Janine set up her own apartment. We remember how happy you were that it was only a few blocks away. You shared a special closeness. We always felt that you had a sixth sense that let you know what Janine was feeling and Janine, too, was finely tuned your feelings. You two were some pair. Sometimes, during your r evening calls, Janine would mention that she had nothing good to snack on in her apartment. And lo and behold, who would show up, good old Mom, bearing gifts of ice cream or cookies. Janine loved to do the mother-daughter things, like going out for dinner or shopping. You always said your daughter had a knack for planning and was able to make every occasion special.

How you loved spending time with your daughters. And we realized that you were not only a great mother but you were a good friend, too.

And then, with both of your daughters settled and on their own, you and Daddy were back as a couple. After 35 years of marriage, you were still devoted to each other.

You worked as a billing supervisor for Ohrenstein and Brown and a few years prior to 2001, you relocated with them to their new home on the 85th floor of the World Trade Center, right after the first bombing attack. You loved working in the buildings. It was a city within the city and you loved your job. Once, your sister-in-law asked you if you were frightened to work at the Twin Towers and you answered in your typical way. "Every morning before I go to work I ask the Lord to be with me and then I leave for work." I am sure on September 11, your 58th birthday, you did ask God to be with you and trust He was there to take your hand and lead you home.

Knowing you as well as Felicia did she feels you would have liked to leave us with a special message. She found this verse that was written years ago by H.S. Holland, Canon of St. Paul's Cathedral, in London. She thinks it expressed what you would say to us . . . .

Death is nothing at all; I have only slipped away into the next room.

I am I, and you are you; whatever we were to each other, that we still are. Call me by my familiar name; speak to me in the easy way you always used. Put no difference into you tone; wear no forced air of solemnity or sorrow. Laugh as we always laughed at the little jokes we enjoyed together. Play, smile, and think of me. Pray for me. Life means all that it ever meant. It is the same as it always was; there is absolutely unbroken continuity. I am but waiting for you, for an interval, somewhere very near, just around the corner . . . . All is well.

And, by the way, Janine has finally married Teddy and you have two additional grandsons, Demetri and Marco, who were cheated the opportunity to meet you, but know so much about you and love you very much.

Yes Mom . . . . we miss you . . . . we love you . . . . FOREVER IN OUR HEARTS!!!

We love you up to the sky and all around the moon.

Maria-Elena and Janine

JASON CHRISTOPHER DeFAZIO

Jason Christopher DeFazio was born on July 12, 1972 in Staten Island, New York to James and Roseann DeFazio. He is the brother of Michael James DeFazio and the Uncle to Alexis Michele, Ariana Rose and Jaden Elizabeth DeFazio. He married Michele Moss on June 23, 2001. Jason graduated from Curtis High School in 1991 where he played football. He was studying business at the College of Staten Island. He worked his way up from the mailroom and became a bonds trader for Cantor Fitzgerald. However, Jason planned on joining the NYC Fire Department and received word of his acceptance shortly after September 11th. He studied boxing and martial arts. Jason was on the 103rd floor in the North Tower on September 11th. He was 29 years old.

Roseann DeFazio (Mother)
Age: 59

Our Dear Son Jay,

To put onto paper our feelings almost ten years later still is—and always will be—hard. You mean the world to us and life without you just stinks. You were this handsome guy that looked like a model and had this simile that would light up a room. You loved your family and loved your friends. Your bonds of friendship grew from kids hanging out to wonderful men. The fact that you had so many friends tells me that I raised a wonderful person who loved many but, more importantly, who was loved by so many.

Your family was so important to you that there wasn't anything you wouldn't do for them. If Dad, your brother, or I needed you, you were always there for us. Alexis was your first niece and you loved her so much. You were like a second dad to her. You took her everywhere. She misses you a lot now. Your brother, Mike, misses you so much, too. I hear him say how he wishes you could come down and talk to him just once more. I think we all wish we could have just one more moment to say we love you.

I guess you can say one thing: never take life for granted because you never know what could happen. I know that you lived each day to the fullest and that you enjoyed each day that you had. I also know that you wanted to buy a house and have a life with your wife, Michele. You told me that on Sunday, just two days before 9/11. You even showed me a house right up the block from my brother, Anthony, which was for sale.

I remember that Sunday I was going to work and I didn't get to spend time with you. Who knew what was coming? I know that you are with my Dad and you loved Grandpa so much. Sometimes when I am having a bad day I wish I were with you too, but only for a second, because I know that they need me here. Michael, Alexis and your Dad need me here, even though

I'm the butt of all of his jokes. Your niece, Ariana, always asks for you and I tell her all about you. She named her new baby brother Aiden Jay after you. She is getting to know who you were because I tell her about you.

I remember your wedding day. I couldn't wait to dance with you to the song, *A Song for My Son on His Wedding Day*. The day was like a big party. You and Michele were so happy and I was so happy for you. I don't believe I will ever be that happy again.

I lost part of myself when I lost you. I think each one of us feels the same way. You gave us so much love we miss it, as much as we miss you. I know when it is time will be together again.

All Our Love

Mom, Dad, Michael, Alexis, Ariana, Jaden, and Dee

SCOTT McGOVERN

Scott Martin McGovern was born on November 29, 1965 in Brooklyn, New York to Elisabeth Scott and Martin McGovern, the brother to Tara. Scott married Jill Shaffro in 1995 and they had two children, Alana and Nicole. Scott earned a B.S in Business from SUNY Albany, and had completed two of the three levels to become a Chartered Financial Analyst. Scott worked for Cantor Fitzgerald and moved to Eurobrokers in September 2001. He loved his children, his wife, his friends and his family with all of his heart. Scott was an Oakland Raiders fan, played golf and enjoyed the company of his friends. On September 11, 2001, Scott was at his desk on the 84th floor of the South Tower. He was 35 years old.

Nicole McGovern (Daughter)
Age: 11

Alana McGovern (Daughter)
Age: 14

Dear Daddy,

Although I can't remember all the things we did together,
I still know the memories we've shared will last forever.
You've always taught me right from wrong,
And in our few years together, our bond grew very strong.

You have always loved all of us so dearly,
And we all miss you a lot, clearly.
Going through all of this has sometimes made me sad,
But knowing that you're always here with me makes it not so bad.

I hope you're proud of me from everything I do,
And I try to help others, just like you.
You were always a great Dad,
And when I think about you, I am always glad.

I hope you get this message even from up above,
And I want you to know I send you all of my love.

Love,
Nicole

Dear Dad,

The Secret Park

Slippery Slides,
Worn out handlebars,
Rusted picnic tables,
Memories remain.
The swings are pendulums,
The heart of a grandfather clock,
Swish, swish, swish,
Back and forth, forth and back.

The slides are tunnels
That lead to a mysterious
Land that only kids
Can discover,
Slip, slip, slip
Into the darkness.

The dog from across
The street yelps,
Wishing he could play, too.
He knows he can't though,
Because secret park
Is just for me and my dad,
Bark, bark, bark
Sorry dog, you can't come.

Though during school hours
Elementary school students run about
The premises,
At dusk when the kids
Are eating dinner, and the
Teachers are grading papers . . .
My dad and me,
Me and my dad
Are playing
At our secret park.

JAMES MICHAEL GARTENBERG

James Michael Gartenberg was born on December 23, 1965 in Manhattan to parents Irving and Lois Gartenberg, brother of Julie. He married Jill Freeberg in November 1994. Jim and Jill had daughter Nicole in 1999. Jill was three months pregnant with their second child when Jim died on September 11th. Jamie Michelle, Jim's namesake, was born in March 2002. Jim dedicated 12 years as the president of the University Of Michigan Club Of New York. There is now a scholarship at The University of Michigan which affords a New York City student the opportunity to attend the University of Michigan, a place Jim held very dear to his heart (he received his B.A in 1987). One of Jim's favorite activities was attending University of Michigan football games with friends. Jim was a loyal friend, husband, father, son and brother. There are few people as kind-hearted, fun and quick-witted as Jim. He worked as a real estate broker for Juilen J. Studley Inc. Jim was last heard from on the 86th floor of Tower 1, WTC. He was 35 years young.

Jill Gartenberg Pila (Wife)
Age: 44

Nicole Holly Gartenberg Pila (Daughter)
Age: 12

Dear Jimmy,

Our daughter, Jamie, has your quick wit, great sense of humor and love for life. I was only three months pregnant with her when you died on that fateful day. We knew we were going to be blessed with another child but we didn't know she was going to be a girl. She is your namesake (Jamie Michelle for James Michael) and she is the special gift you left for me. I love her more than words can say and I'm so sad that you're not here to see how amazing she is.

When Jamie was in preschool, the teacher had the moms come in the class for "Mother's Day Tea." She asked us to go around the room and talk about why our child is so special to us . . . when they got to me I didn't know where to begin . . . I simply said (as I was all choked up with emotion) that Jamie is the special gift you left for me when you were killed on September 11th.

Nicole was only 2 ½ years old when you passed away, but she truly remembers you and that moment in time. Just days after 9/11, Nicole asked if she could watch you and me in our wedding video—she wanted to see you alive and happy. It was then that I knew that she truly understood. Her Daddy was gone. We watched that video over and over and over for years. We have since made a photo album of the two of you. Ten years later, Nicole still treasures that book and the memories within it. She's savored learning every detail of every picture. She also cherishes the knowledge of who you were.

Just after you passed away, I asked friends and loved ones to please write letters about you, so that Nicole and Jamie would come to understand what a special, selfless person you were. I have all of those letters in a book. I'm so thankful to everyone who shared memories with us.

There are certain memories of you that I hold dear to my heart. Whenever we'd walk in the city you would always give change to the homeless people on the streets. I couldn't believe you gave to every single one every single time. And your response was simply, "We have more than they do." You always saw the best in people; you never passed judgments. That's a quality very few people possess. If more people were like you, there'd be a lot more peace in this world.

Of course, there are the memories of your love of the University of Michigan. As the President of the NYC Alumni Chapter for 12 years, your passion for the University of Michigan was clear! We'd go to football games every year—and once Nicole was born, of course she, too, joined in the fun (although for baby Nicole it was more LOUD than fun!). You'll be happy to know, she does *now* appreciate the U of M!

It was only fitting that when you passed away we created a scholarship in your name at the University of Michigan. The scholarship is almost a full scholarship as we continue to fundraise for the James M. Gartenberg Memorial Scholarship Fund. Particularly active is your close friend, Adam Goldman, who holds an annual golf outing in your honor with the proceeds going to the scholarship. You'll be happy to know that one criteria for the scholarship is that the student must be a New York City native. I have been in constant contact with each recipient every year and they are so appreciative of the scholarship. You'd be so proud.

In 2004, I remarried. My new husband has qualities similar to those you possessed—he, too, is kind-hearted, selfless and warm. Jay was widowed with two children (he lost his wife under different circumstances). We connected as soon as we met. We both felt as if you and his late wife were pulling strings from above—if you couldn't be with me, then you and his late wife would want us to be happy and have our children be a part of a family. It wasn't simply that I "met someone else" as everyone said I would. It's deeper than that.

When we got married I moved out to New Jersey. I know, I know, we weren't leaving Manhattan for anything, but when life threw that curve ball, we just never know where it's going to take us next. I closed my private practice in the city and sold our apartment. We bought a house together to start over as a "blended" family. Nicole and Jamie understand that you are their biological father and the genes they have from you are very strong (if you could only see a picture of Nicole and Jamie—they're ALL you!). Your mom is still part of our lives, she visits the kids and they visit her. We are truly still a family. We talk about you often and love to see photos of you . . . there are just so many memories that make me laugh . . . you were always so good at making me laugh . . . and I can still laugh to this day.

I'm glad I got to say "goodbye" to you. Although I wanted to be hopeful the several times we spoke that morning ten years ago, I knew, although in disbelief, that you, and many others, were not going to make it out of there alive. The world is changed forever. Every day.

I love you Jimmy. And I miss you so.

XO
Jill

Dear Daddy,

I miss you so much! You were funny, caring, kind, and an amazing dad to me. When you died, I was still little, which meant I didn't know exactly what was going on at the time. Now that I am older, I have really thought about what happened to you and that is the most terrible thing that could happen to anyone—especially someone as kind and caring as you. Even though I was with you for a very short amount of time, we have so many great and unforgettable memories that will last forever.

You made me who I am today. I love and miss you!

Love always,
Nicole

ROBERT LOUIS SCANDOLE

Robert Louis Scandole was born on February 9, 1965 in Brooklyn, New York, to Robert and Margaret Scandole, the brother of Christopher. He married Sheila O'Grady in 1991 and they have two daughters, Emma and Katie. Robert earned a BA and an MBA from St. John's University and worked for Cantor Fitzgerald. His greatest love was his family. He was a diehard New York Knicks fan and Mets fan. He enjoyed his summers at Breezy Point and especially Sundays at The Sugarbowl. On September 11, 2001, Robert was at his desk on the 104th floor in the North Tower. He was 36 years old.

Sheila Scandole (Wife)
Age: 46

Katie Scandole (Daughter)
Age: 12

Dear Rob,

I am writing this letter almost ten years after that unforgettable fall day. Sometimes I feel like it was a lifetime ago and other times it feels as though it just happened yesterday. There is not a morning, afternoon or evening that goes by that you don't come into my thoughts. It's usually me thinking that you would have really enjoyed something, or you would have been so proud of the girls, or just how much I miss you. Sometimes I look up at the night's sky and wonder where you are. I know you are looking down at me. I always knew that our love was special and rare and now I know that it is endless.

Even though my heart aches for you, I am most sad for Emma and Katie, that they do not have you in their lives. I know you would have been at every one of their games as the assistant head coach of all their teams just like you said you would, because you didn't want to be the mean head coach. You would have been beside me at every milestone in their lives and beaming with pride and joy. When I look at fathers and daughters, I always think that would have been you giving the piggyback rides, holding hands, playing basketball, skiing together, playing in the water and riding bikes. Emma and Katie would have been the luckiest girls to have a dad like you who would spoil, support, encourage, guide and love them always. Even though they had you for such a short time, I always tell them that I have never seen a father who loved his children more than you did. They were your whole life and nothing was more important to you than your family.

I am so blessed to have Emma and Katie. You are living in them. People say that Emma looks like me but I see you in her. She is beautiful inside and out. She is smart, funny, strong willed, sensitive and outgoing. She has that zest for living life to the fullest just like you did. She recently had to write an essay for school which she used the quote "Dream as if you'll live forever, and live as if you'll die today." I thought it was so you. Katie is just as beautiful. I think she looks like you. When she sleeps, she does the same as you did, putting her arm over her head. I watch her sleep and I always smile. She has your long eyelashes, too. Katie is also a bright, determined, conscientious student, athletic, funny, and a good little girl. She was very shy as a baby and she now has this enormous personality with so much life. Even though our hearts will never completely heal, time has made our hearts less heavy. It is easier for me now to talk about you and share all of your silly things that you did. I even think our friends talk more about you now. They love hearing the funny stories from when you were a teenager, those famous college years, and Sunday afternoons at the Sugar Bowl. I know that you are smiling from heaven because Emma and Katie are now friends with your friend's children from Breezy Point. You always said there was nothing like your Breezy friends.

Emma turned fourteen and applied to an all-girls high school. I know you would have wanted that. I used that to persuade her decision. She plays volleyball, basketball and tennis. She is in the drama club and chorus. She just finished the production of *Godspell* at her school and she was great in it. She is also an honor student. She is amazing.

Katie is twelve and started middle school and is very popular. She plays basketball, softball and tennis. She made the honor roll. She even participated in the production of *Grease Jr*.

Our family has helped and supported me in raising Emma and Katie and I could not have done it without them. I think Emma and Katie love your mom and dad as much as a person would love a parent. They are so lucky to have them as grandparents. Chris and Annemarie have taught the girls how to ski. They go to Hunter whenever they can. Chris will only take them skiing on Hunter Mountain, just like you would have wanted. Mary-Jo and Maura have always filled in whenever I needed them. They are always willing to listen, love, guide and support the girls.

As for me, I was so fortunate to be loved by you. You were such a gift to me. I hope Emma, Katie and myself will live life like you did, living each day to the fullest and always doing the right thing. My hope for all of us is peace and happiness. Until we meet again.

Love Always,
Sheila

Dear Dad,

I miss you more than words can ever explain. These long years without you left me wondering what it would have been like to have you here. No matter what happens, no one can ever replace you as my dad.

I have accomplished many things and it saddens me that you can never be here to share in my future accomplishments. People can say that they understand the way I feel inside, but they don't. It hurts me to see other kids with their dad and playing catch outside, knowing that I can never experience all of these wonderful things. I often pray to God asking him to watch over our family and to even send messages to you that I tell him. I was so little when this tragedy happened. I wasn't old enough to grasp the concept that you were gone and that you were never coming back. Now that I understand, I frequently think about all of the memories that people have told me about you. I cannot tell you how many times I couldn't stop sobbing over what has happened.

On September 11th every year, I go to church but I only stay there for a few minutes. I am too depressed. I leave with my cousins and go to the memorial they built. I could sit there for hours and ponder all of the things that you and I shared. I've seen all of the pictures that Grandma and Grandpa found. There were at least 100 of them. You seemed like the exact same person I am now as a kid. My favorite picture had to be of you and Uncle Chris when you were playing the piano with just cowboy hats on. I remember when we went to Disney World. I was either too small or too scared to go on any of the rides.

Everybody told me that there was nothing you loved more than your family. Dad, I just want you to know that I love you more than life itself. All I want is for you to be proud of me. I feel like a part of me is missing. Even though you're not beside me right now, you will forever live in my heart. All of the memories I can never have with you hurts me inside.

But I also know that you wouldn't want me to dwell on the horrible thing that happened. So I just want to tell you some of the things that have been going on. I play basketball, softball, tennis, and ski. I continue to take my weekly visits to Breezy and spend all of my summer there. I am now 12 years-old. We got a dog named Wags and I have a turtle. Emma and Mom are doing fine and inspire me every day with the examples they set for me in life. You are missed, and in your favorite place, there are pictures reminding everybody of your spectacular times. You were a great husband, son, uncle, brother, cousin, nephew and most off all, the best father any girl could ever ask for.

By the way, I am a Mets fan and I know that you would be proud!

I really can't describe how much I miss and love you. I am at a loss for words. I hope that this letter can at least give you an idea about how much I love you. Although I won't see you, you will always be in my heart.

Your loving daughter,
Katie

ARTHUR JOSEPH JONES III

Arthur Joseph Jones III was born June 25, 1964 in Brooklyn, New York, and was later joined by his two brothers, Scott and Peter. Arthur attended Hamilton College and upon graduation was New York City bound—employed by Dean Witter as a stock trader, subsequently advancing with Carr Futures located in the World Trade Center North Tower, 91st floor. He married Carol Francolini and they had four children, Julia, Charlotte, Harry, Joseph, the last born in April of 2002. Arthur was a "Renaissance" man, who enjoyed cooking, New York theater, sports, listening to all forms of music (his favorite was jazz) or attending NASCAR events, the Kentucky and Belmont Derbys with family, clients or friends. On September 11th, he was working for Carr Futures in the North Tower. He was 37 years old.

Marilyn Stufano (Mother)
Age: 67

Dear Arthur:

Your presence did not go unnoticed as you could bring friends, acquaintances and strangers together and by the end of the day everyone felt like old friends. Your great smile greeted all of us and when we spent time in your company; we always wanted more time with you. We were your "moment in time" as you gave us your undivided attention. You would extend your large embracing hand to connect with ours and then extend your other arm and hand to hold on to our shoulder to "take us all". Yes, you sure did take us all in!

I so miss your physical charismatic presence and, thinking of you each day, I sometimes struggle with my sadness. However, accepting, forgiving and continuing to make this world a better place is what you would want me to do. And so each day I am committed to this end. "Let there be peace on earth and let it begin with me".

I continue to see and feel your presence in spirit in this world as reflected in the laugh of a child, a music piece, a gift of nature and most especially in my moments of meditation and prayer. The "Great Physician" who is God continues to mend the hole left in my heart the day you left this world. My faith sustains me in God's promise of Eternal Life. Let us not dwell on the tragedy of September 11th, 2001. Instead, think of all the love and acts of unselfish kindness for in so doing we will continue to honor our loved ones who lost their lives. Let us continue to promote love and random acts of kindness and promote world peace.

Your family and friends have—and will continue to—celebrate your life. We are all born to shine each in our own special way and your life was meaningful and will always be celebrated.

Your good friend, Jenny, sent this to me after we lost you. She said you wrote it back in 1982.

"THE FUTURE HOLDS"

We say good luck to each other
Where are we headed?
In which direction.
Who knows; it's magical.
That's what true life holds:
The ability to forgive and forget.
We wonder why things work.
It's not magical; it's simply predestined.
Everything is meant to be.
Someday everyone will see
That it's the person inside the person.
Cry and remember about good times
"Cause things will surely pick up."

It's not different.
It's the same.
Same old Story
What's new?
Just our atmospheres!

Love is love
Regardless of distance.
It should not matter
If it's really present.

Where are we going?
What direction?
Who knows; it's exciting, different.
Who cares,
Fun is fun but life starts soon
We're full of dares.

Your choice is a tough one.
You've made your own choice.
Things can only get better
Than before.
Hopefully smiles will resound
When smiles are tough to bring.

You were the best. You did make this world a better place. Let us all go forth and make our world shine with love and peace.

I thank God for His gift to me of you and the honor of nurturing and sharing your life in this world as your mother.

Love, Mom

RICHARD WOODWELL

Richard Herron Woodwell was born in Pittsburgh, Pennsylavnia on June 18th, 1957, to Knowles and Martha Woodwell, the brother of JK and Pam. He married Linda Preston in 1988 in San Francisco and they have three children, Richard, Margaret and Eleanor. Richard earned a BA from Dartmouth College and worked for Keefe, Bruyette and Woods. He loved his family, playing golf and spending time in Hyannis Port, Massachusetts. On September 11th, Richard was at his desk on the 182nd floor in World Trade II. He was 44 years old.

Linda Woodwell (Wife)
Age: 56

Dear Richard,

I would love to be throwing you a birthday party every year, probably a golf outing. Instead, I reflect on who you were, what you accomplished and what you gave to the people around you. You had a strong and gracious spirit. You loved life and lived it to its fullest.

In September of 1971, you entered Avon Old Farms School as a freshman. You always said that it was Avon that pointed you in the direction that shaped the rest of your life. Avon was a very inspirational school and you loved it. It incorporated core values into everyday curricula and lives of the boys who attended. Your life reflected these values of integrity, scholarship, civility, altruism, tolerance sportsmanship, self-discipline and social responsibility. You demonstrated these values throughout your life in your relationships with family, friends and colleagues.

I started the *Richard Woodwell Scholarship Fund* at Avon Old Farms in 2001 to honor you. The scholarship helps young men attend Avon who otherwise would not be able to. My hope is that this opportunity will shape other young men the way it did you.

Miss you and love you.

Love,
Linda, Richard, Margaret and Eleanor

RICHARD BLAINE MADDEN

Richard Blaine Madden was born on June 30, 1966 in Elgin, Illinois, to Robert and Michelle Madden, the brother of Robert, Joshua, Mark and Melissa. He married Maura McIntyre in 1996 and their daughter Patricia was born on February 17, 2000. Richard earned a BA from Denison University and a J.D. from New York Law School. He worked for AON. He loved his wife, daughter, parents, siblings, extended family and many friends. On September 11th, Richard was at this desk on the 100th floor of the South Tower. He was 35 years old.

Tricia Madden Lezynski (Daughter)
Age: 12

Dear Daddy,

It seems so hard to believe that nearly ten years have passed since I last hugged you. I've changed a lot since that day and I am quickly growing up. I talk much more now than I did then. I know many things now I did not know then. I have learned what an incredible human being the world lost on that September day.

One of my favorite pictures of you and I together is the one of us walking down our street, you holding my hand, guiding me. I was barely walking then and the picture only shows us from behind, but I can feel our connection. Your big hand reaching down to my small fingers. It's black and white and seems as if it might have been taken yesterday except for the fact I'm much taller now than when it was taken.

Daddy, I want you to know that even though you are not physically by my side, you are still holding my hand in spirit every day. You are with me most importantly in the way Mommy loves me and raises me. You are with me whenever we see Grandmom, Uncle Bob, Uncle Mark, Uncle Josh and Aunt Melissa. You are with me whenever we visit with our Crowley cousins. You are with me whenever we see your old friends. Aggie, Red, T, Duck, Bake, and Pudge have made sure to stay in touch. I am so thankful that everyone tells me stories about you. There are stories about you at all different ages and they are all funny.

Mom reminds me that you would also be very proud of me. I am a very good student, athlete and friend. My last report card, I missed straight A's by one B+. Last softball season, our team went to the championship game only to lose in the last inning. Same with swimming, our team finished in second and I was named most improved swimmer. I have lots of friends both at school and outside of school. I wish they could meet you. They would be impressed with how tall and handsome you are, how kind and smart you are. Most importantly, like you, I have a good caring heart.

You may have gone to heaven, but you will forever be at my side both in heart and spirit. I admire you, miss you, but most importantly, I love you Daddy.

Love,
Tricia

STEPHEN HUCZKO

Stephen Huczko was born December 15, 1956 to Stephen and Elizabeth Huczko. He was the oldest child and had three siblings: Richard, Mary Beth, and David. Stephen married Kathleen McGuire in 1982, and together they had four children: Kaitlyn, Liam, Cullen, and Aidan. Steve was a proud officer of the Port Authority Police Department and, in 1992, he returned to school for a nursing degree while working nights. He graduated RVCC School of Nursing in 1995 as a Registered Nurse. Steve enjoyed all things athletic from running (he completed the NYC Marathon in 2000) to bike riding and hiking with his family, as well as cooking and spending any free time he had with family and friends. He enjoyed life to the fullest. On the morning of September 11, 2001, Steve had just reported for duty at the Jersey City Port Authority Tech Center, located at the New Jersey entrance to the Holland Tunnel. He was one of the first responders on the scene at the North Tower. Five months later his remains were recovered just 24 inches from the exit door of the North Tower, along with four fellow officers, and a civilian woman strapped in a rescue chair. He was 44 years old.

Kaitlyn Huczko, 27; Liam Huczko, 23; Cullen Huczko, 17; and Aidan Huczko, 15 (children)

Dear Deeda,

We have all grown quite a lot since we last saw you. As we reflect on the ups and downs of the past ten years, we realize that although you weren't able to raise us in person, you were there in memory and in spirit, constantly molding us into the people we are today. If there comes a time when we can all reunite, you will probably be proud to find all of the ways we've taken after you. While we have learned many individual lessons from you, here are just a few:

"I learned to try anything once."

"I learned how to eat sunflower seeds by the handful."

"I learned that meeting new people is one of life's greatest joys."

"I learned that cheap beer is not a shameful thing."

"I learned how to tell a good story."

"I learned how to steer the car with my knees."

"I learned to cook healthy, delicious meals."

"I learned that the people with whom you choose to surround yourself can become as close as family."

"I learned that there is no surer path to success than hard work."

"I learned that I will always hit a deer at the worst possible time."

"I learned that listening makes you a trusted friend."

"I learned that people don't always have 'the good' in them, but to never stop trying to find it."

"I learned that sleep is overrated."

"I learned to love working out."

"I learned that my eyes are powerful weapons."

"I learned to always laugh at my mistakes."

"I learned that my favorite place to be is behind the camera."

"I learned to love unusual food."

"I learned how wonderful hats are."

"I learned to draw a pretty killer portrait."

"I learned to save the punch line for last."

"I learned to teach gently and with lots of encouragement."

"I learned to seize the day."

Thanks for being the man and father that you were. While this short passage doesn't begin to express the scope of our love and gratitude, we hope it shows you that our lives are infinitely richer for having you in them, even for such a short while. We promise always to honor your memory, and to share with others the many ways you expressed your irrepressible zeal for life.

We love you forever,
Aidan, Cullen, Liam, and Kaitlyn

WILLIAM JOHN ERWIN

William John Erwin, Billy, as he was known to his family and friends, was born in Brooklyn, New York on October 15, 1970. He is predeceased by his mother and father, Joan and John Erwin and survived by his stepmother, Lorraine Erwin, his aunt Teresa Slanina, his wife Eileen Erwin and his son Brendan Erwin. He graduated with honors from S.U.N.Y. Plattsburgh with a BA in Economics. He started working at Cantor Fitzgerald in 1997. He had a passion for BMX biking and rugby and he was a diehard Yankee and Giants fan and loved being a New Yorker. Billy met his wife, Eileen, in July of 1990 and they married August 8, 1997 and had a son, Brendan, on June 20, 2001. Billy was working alongside his best friends on the 105th floor of One World Trade Center on September 11th. He was 30 years old.

Brendan Erwin (Son)
Age: 10

Dear Daddy,

The day it happened, when only three months old, may change the way you look, see, or hear. 9/11. The time my father's life ended and my heart shattered. Just one more hug would make my day.

Love,
Brendan

GARRY W. LOZIER

Garry Westervelt Lozier, son of Patricia M. Lozier and Raymond W. Lozier, was born on January 4, 1954 in Hackensack, New Jersey. Garry grew up in Closter, New Jersey and graduated from the Dwight–Englewood School in Englewood before attending Lehigh University, where he graduated with a degree in Finance in 1978. He met his wife Kathy while attending a wedding in Jackson Hole, Wyoming, and they were married in May 1990. Garry loved to ski and could be found on the slopes with his three children, Evan, Karoline and Olivia during winter weekends. He finished three New York City Marathons in his life, and enjoyed running, biking, windsurfing and coaching his son Evan's hockey team. He was a devoted and compassionate husband, father, and brother to his two sisters, Ann Lozier Rhorborn, and Christie Lozier Heilmann. On Sept 11, 2001 Garry was at his Managing Director's desk at Sandler O'Neill and Partners on the 104th floor of the South Tower. He was 47 years old.

Kathleen Lozier (Wife)
Age: 53

Garry,

Today we're remembering you for your wide-beaming smile and the sparkle in your eye. We're lucky because your intense love of life and your natural ability to make everyone around you laugh somehow genetically planted itself into your three children.

We miss your incredible mind, and your ability to explain ancient world history, the inverted yield curve, and the rhythm of the waves of the ocean to all of us in one conversation. We miss sharing the outdoors with you and your deep love of nature and animals.

We miss your ability to see the positive in any situation, and we could have used a cache of your "upbeat attitude pep talks" on some of our darkest days over the past ten years. We miss your enthusiasm for life, and your energy. Most of all, though, we miss the dedication and love that you had for all of us.

Although time is said to "heal," time also puts you further from our lives. What time has given us, is the ability to reflect—to ask why? To work through our disbelief over the heinous crimes committed on September 11, 2001. Time has given us the ability to better accept and work through our anger, our sadness, and the loneliness we had to overcome without you here.

With the passage of time, we have been able to look toward the positive again. Birthdays and wedding anniversaries have passed, bones have been broken, and graduations without you have been bittersweet; our faces streaming with tears of joy mixed with tears of sadness that you didn't live to see the day. Christmases have come and gone, as have two sets of braces. We know that you wouldn't want us to be sad, and we do our best to be happy here on earth without you.

We still miss you, and we know in our hearts that you would want us to find the beauty and the positive in our lives again, and we've chosen to do so.

Love,
Kathy, Evan, Karoline and Olivia

WILLIAM FALLON JR.

William Lawrence Fallon Jr. was born on September 20, 1962, on Long Island, New York, to William Sr. and Elizabeth Fallon, and was the brother of Elizabeth and Kenneth. He earned a BS in Computer Science from the Polytechnic Institute of New York in 1984 and an MS in Computer Science from the New York Institute of Technology in 1991. He married his high school sweetheart, Laura Wesely, on June 16, 1984, and lived in Coram, New York. Their daughter, Kathleen, was born on July 12, 1990, and Kayla was born on May 29, 1993. Bill's interests included running, cycling, travel and anything that involved fun with his daughters. He was Manager of Technical Support for Cantor Fitzgerald and was in his office on the 103rd floor of the North Tower on September 11. He was thirty-nine years old.

Kathleen Fallon (Daughter)
Age: 21

Hey Daddy,

I want to tell people: Have you ever felt a building sway? I have. Do you know how small taxis look when you are 103 floors up? I do. Do you know the exact time to jump when an elevator is about to stop, so it feels like you're flying? No? I did and more before the age of 11, because you had the best job at the coolest place in the whole entire world.

Remember those days in the city, waking up super early to catch the train, and going to the donut man for breakfast? You used to always let me play on the extra computer; who knows what I must have done to that thing? You had that white board in your office and it was so much fun to draw on. Also, getting lunch and sitting by the palm trees in the Winter Garden, then having some chocolate chip Italian ices and eating them in front of the fountain.

Remember those trips you took us on? Did you ever think how much they would affect me? We walked across the Continental Divide, down the Grand Canyon, up many mountains, around geysers, and swam under the sea. Who knew I would devote my life to studying these things? I'm in college now, aren't you proud of me? And I have you to thank for everything because you pushed me in the right direction and even though I had to grow up without you, you influenced the most important part of my life.

Remember those nights at home? I miss your chicken enchiladas, I haven't had one since you have been gone. You always had a milkshake for me when you picked me up from dance and who knew McDonald's had so many flavors? We loved to sing, even though both of us knew we can't; blasting the radio to our song singing along to "Takin' Care of Business" on our way to the library. I've outgrown my baseball mitt and my pink football was thrown out many years ago, but I still root for our Mets. You used to take me to the YMCA every Saturday for swim lessons and now I am the one teaching those same lessons to new kids. You tried to teach me how to skateboard, and now I can put a skateboard together, even though I still can't ride one!

I'm grown now and I drive a car that I own. I've had more jobs than I can count on one hand. I am looking at graduate schools to apply to. I even have a credit card! I am still, and always will be, your little girl and it hurts every day not having you here with me to hold my hand and help me stay on the slippery dangerous trail that is life, like you used to when we would hike out west.

I love you so much and miss you every day.

Gotcha Back,
Kathleen

CIRA MARIE PATTI

Cira Marie Patti was born April 21, 1961 in Brooklyn, New York. Her parents were Michael and Frances Patti. Cira Marie had two younger brothers, Michael and Richard, along with her younger sister Juliann. She was very devoted to her two nieces and god child, Michael. An avid sports fan, Cira attended most Yankees and Giants games. Cira worked for KBW on the 89th floor of the South Tower of the WTC. She was 40 years old.

Michael and Frances Patti (Parents)
Ages: 71 and 66

Dear Cira,

September 11th, 2001 was a beautiful day. Close to 300 people went to work that day and never realized that it would be their last day on Earth. On Monday night, the day before, it was football time at the Meadowlands. The New York Giants were playing—Opening Day. You were such an ardent Giants fan and would attend most home games as you did that night. The next day it was off to work. You made two phone calls to us, as was the norm. The first one at home, the second when you arrived at work.

We were at home the morning of September 11th watching the morning news on television. Along came a flash on the screen showing the North Tower at the World Trade Center in flames. Apparently, a stray airliner had crashed into the building, causing serious damage. We immediately called you, being very concerned, as you worked on the 89th floor of the South Tower, preparing to start work at 9:00 am. Oddly enough, many of the workers had no idea what had happened at the North Tower. The Port Authority, via the speaker system, assured you to stay put in your building, which would keep you out of harm's way. Reluctantly, you did not leave your workplace. At approximately 8:05, our phone rang and it was you. In the background, you could hear screaming and panic. The South Tower was hit by a second hijacked plane. Unfortunately, it was below the 89th floor. Your last words to us were, "Help me, the walls and floors are falling." And then there was silence.

To hear a child reaching out to her parents for help and not being able to help her, is very hard to live with. We never received any remains, along with 1,200 other families. At present, there are thousands of remains at the Medical Examiners in New York City. Present day DNA is not able to match positive identification; hopefully, future progress will be made in that field.

You loved the water, so we made sure we obtained a cemetery plot overlooking the bay in Staten Island. The plot still remains empty. A memorial mass was held for you at Holy Child Parish in Staten Island. The church was filled with so many friends and family. It was a very touching ceremony.

We belong to a support group in Staten Island on Wednesday nights. A very strong bond has developed with other family members who also lost their loved ones on that terrible day. You were a resident of Staten Island, as we were, before we moved to New Jersey. Traveling to Manhattan every September 11th, renews the sad times that we all had to endure. Reading the names of all the victims is something we all do, which is a sad but rewarding thing. Ten years have gone by since that awful day. Time does not heal the suffering; it is something that will never go away.

Working among the most chatty and virtually adept members of institutional sales, your one-line responses were well renowned. As an administrative assistant for KBW's equity sales desk, you were never at a loss for words. And you often surprised your colleagues with sarcasm and quick comebacks. You were known to challenge anyone with your own opinions, whether it regarded sports or life. You were always correct in any squabble. This made you one of the most popular people on the desk.

You spent your last twenty years working in Manhattan. You enjoyed the best that New York had to offer in your free time including plays, shows, and dinners. You enjoyed life; you lived out a New York life.

You were 40 years old at the time of your death. Being single, you spent much time with your nephew and nieces, helping them with their homework, reports, shopping and sports, which you enjoyed doing so much. You were always there for us, whether it be shopping or taking us to the doctors or other appointments.

You always made a point of stressing the fact that you will always be there for us when we grew old. Unfortunately, that never came to be.

Summer weekends it was off to the big rental house at Bradley Beach, New Jersey. Anchoring your evenings was the Columns, a Victorian place on Ocean in Avon by the Sea whose white Russians met your standards. You would dance or hold your own debates on the Mets or the Yankees or Eric Clapton, all of which made part of your chain.

Holidays, it was in our kitchen where nephews, nieces, sisters and brothers and Aunt CeeCee soared. Your pasta sauce was not just about garlic and tomatoes. Of course not. This was "Italian" sauce." We recall the spices, the sausage, pork, beef, and meatballs. That was your day; that was Christmas.

We miss you and love you so much.

Love,
Mom and Dad

BERNARD FAVUZZA

Bernard Favuzza was born on April 13, 1949 to Domenick and Vincenza Favuzza. He was the brother of Janice Favuzza and Annamarie Favuzza. Bernard was raised in Ridgewood, Queens where he met and married his wife, Linda Denhoff, in 1969. Bernard has two daughters, Donna Favuzza Posta and Laura Favuzza Bittel. He began his career in the financial industry at Bankers Trust then moved on to Fundamental Brokers, Inc., RMJ Securities and finally, Cantor Fitzgerald. He was the proud grandfather of Dominick, born in 1999. Since that fateful day, four more grandchildren have arrived: Talia, Lucah, Anthony and Sawyer. On September 11th, Bernard was on the 104th floor of One World Trade Center. He was 52 years old.

Donna Posta (Daughter)
Age: 42

Janice Favuzza and Anna Favuzza (Sisters)
Ages: 59 and 53

Dominick, Talia, Lucah, Anthony and Sawyer (Grandchildren)
Ages: 11, 8, 4, 4, 2

Dear Dad,

You were a wonderful man with a wonderful smile. You were outgoing, funny and you made friends wherever you went. You were a son, a brother, a husband, a father, and most recently, a grandfather. The job you loved most.

You grew up in Queens, New York and were a big ice and roller hockey player in your younger days. When we moved from Queens to Suffern, New York, you became a big Suffern High School hockey fan. You knew all the players and all the parents. Recently, I spoke with a player and I said, "I bet my father always had some piece of advice for how to improve your playing." He replied, "Yes, he always did, and we always listened."

You were a smart man. You were the person I went to for any question I had about anything because if you didn't know the answer you knew someone who did. You were also willing to go out of your way to help people: building a model railroad for a co-worker whose child was suffering from leukemia; helping a new neighbor build his deck; putting in a good word for a friend of mine who was looking for a position in a company where you knew people.

You were also an avid model railroader; a tradition in our family that wasn't so well received by my sister or me. You would spend countless hours working on a giant layout that you yourself said would never be finished. When Dominick, your grandson, was born in 1999, you were so excited. You finally had someone (a boy) to pass down your engineer's cap to. You bought your grandson his first set of trains shortly after his birth and, when he started to take his first steps, you watched intently, anxious for the day you could put him in skates and start teaching him the basics.

You had many friends. The words most often used to describe you are funny, outgoing, honest and smart. We miss you so much now. We miss your smile and your laugh. I especially miss the connection you made with your grandson, Dominick. I miss how happy you were every time you were together.

Can you believe that you now have four grandsons and one granddaughter? We miss you're your wisdom and advice. Every time Dominick (a passionate hockey player) takes the ice, I tear up. This is what you were waiting for; one of your own to cheer on and guide. We can only hope you have that big smile on your face when the oldest scores a goal, when your granddaughter takes the stage for a dance recital, when my sister's oldest is holding court with a bunch of adults because he's the only four year-old I know who can hold a completely intelligible conversation with a crowd of 40 year-olds, when my youngest puts together a train layout and when the youngest of all (almost two) reaches each milestone way ahead of schedule. We've all been robbed of your guidance and wisdom but we continue on without you. We can't help but wonder, what if?

We can only hope that you rest in peace and we will do what we can to keep your spirit and memory alive.

I love you, Dad, and miss you terribly.

Love your daughter,
Donna

Dear Bernard,

Once again, it is a bittersweet feeling we have as we go about putting together a mental album of past, present and future shots of your presence among us. So much has happened to all of us in the last ten years, most of it touched by the memory of that fateful day. Our lives were forever changed, and it has taken most of these years to shake off the horror and go on living some form of normal day to day existence. Your friends constantly regale us with stories of you. You were larger than life to most people who met you. It is a shame that many of the stories only come out after a person's passing. We who knew you the best did not know all there was to you. Our biggest regret is that you are not here to share in the joy of your children raising their children. By the way, they all have something in them that reminds us of you, whether in looks, hobbies, activities or personality. You are still among us in that way. We remember how you called Janice every day after she gave birth to Kevin to monitor his daily progress and later, his newest words or accomplishments. We now feel that we are doing the same with your grandchildren. We keep in touch with cell phones, Internet or Facebook (you would have had to change your outlook on technology as did the rest of us). In closing, please know that we are honored to keep your memory alive and hope that one day we will see you again in that great hockey rink in the sky!

Love,
Janice and Anna

Dear Grandpa Bernie,

We miss you. Even though only one of us was born when you passed away, we all feel like we know you so well, through the stories and pictures of the family. And they tell us we all have a part of you. Dominick loves ice hockey just like you. Talia is an athlete, too. She loves baseball and soccer and even loves making crafts. Lucah, Anthony and Sawyer love the model trains just like you did! We miss you, Grandpa Bernie.

Love,
Dominick, Talia, Lucah, Anthony and Sawyer

THOMAS BRENNAN

Born and raised in Garden City, New York, by John and Anita Brennan, Tom had four siblings: John, Paul, Marybeth and Michael. He was a 1991 graduate of Boston College. He and his wife, Jennifer, had a daughter, Catherine, who was 17 months old at the time of the attack, and a son, Thomas, Jr. who was born on October 24, 2001. Tom cherished time with his family and was an avid music fan. Tom worked for Sandler O'Neill Partners on the 104th floor of the South Tower. He was 32 years old.

Catherine Brennan (Daughter)
Age: 11

I Am Not Grateful He is Dead

Its 9/10/01
Grateful Dead music is blasting
In their big silver Ford.
They are on their way
To buy some furniture
For their brand new house.

The little girl is only eighteen months old
Is dancing
Her dad is smiling.
His short dark brown hair
Is blowing in the wind
From the window

She will be a future #1 fan of the
Grateful Dead
Just like her dad
That's what everybody wanted
After he was gone.

Now that he's no longer here
No more encouragement
No more rides in the car
No more Grateful Dead music
That was their last day together
I miss you dad . . .

JOSEPH JAMES LOSTRANGIO SR.

Joseph James Lostrangio Sr. was born on June 11th, 1953 in Long Island, New York, to James and Anne Lostrangio, the brother of Diane. He married his wife Theresa in 1975 and they had two children, Joseph Jr. and Cathryn. Joseph Sr. earned a law degree from New York Law School and worked in the re-insurance industry as a consultant and advisor. He also established his own company, Synergistic Consultants. He was passionate about many things outside of work, and enjoyed crafting fine cuisine, collecting exotic fish, playing the electric guitar and constantly seeking new challenges and adventures. At the time of his death, Joseph was working for the Devonshire Group in Tower One of the World Trade Center. He was 48 years old.

Cathryn Lostrangio (Daughter)
Age: 26

Dear Daddy,

I miss you so much. I think about all of the good times that we had together. I remember when you were the DJ at my school dance and you brought all your different strobes and lights. I remember how you would paint my nails when Mommy was at work. I remember how we used to go to father/daughter dances and how you would take me to work with you.

I miss you the most when 9/11 comes around. I still remember, it was my first day at my new school (I was attending a private middle school for children with special needs) and we saw what happened on the news and I took out the new business card you gave me and showed it to my teacher. She felt bad for me and I felt very sad. Now when 9/11 comes around I wear one of your old dress shirts with your initials on it and your favorite tie. I wear these things to help me remember you and feel close to you.

When it first happened I had a lot of trouble sleeping because I thought of all the good talks we used to have. We had a very special relationship and I miss that a lot. I still think about you all of the time, Daddy. It was hard for me the first time I had to take a plane after you passed away. Grandma took me, Joseph and Ryan to Ireland as a graduation present. I thought about you a lot when I was on the plane.

I still think about how we used to both put on our chef's shirts and cook all kinds of weird food that you brought home like snake and alligator. You were such a fun guy. We would cook together, play guitar together and you would take me to so many new places. I really, really miss you and wish you were here with me right now.

I love you so much, Daddy.

Love,
Cathryn

BENJAMIN JAMES WALKER

Benjamin James Walker was born on August 2, 1960 to David Walker and Mary Brown, brother of Jane, Ruth and Anne Marie. He married Laura Kenney in 1989 and they had three children, Henry, Christopher and Samantha. Ben worked for Marsh McLellan. He loved his children and his wife, coaching soccer and baseball and cheering on his favorite rugby team, Manchester United. On September 11th, Ben was on the 94th Floor of Tower North. He was 41.

Laura Walker (Wife)

Dear Ben,

Well, I am writing this somewhat under duress because, of course, besides being Grandpa's birthday, today is also the deadline for this submission I have tried to write this in my mind so many times, but it is just way too crowded up there. And then it occurred to me: this deadline really represents everything about what life has been like these past ten years since you've were taken from us far too soon. We've had deadlines for so many things I've lost track. Keeping up has been a full time job! So what is the point of this letter, to complain to you? No, you've heard it all already in my dreams (and sometimes nightmares). The point of this letter is to make sure that the rest of the world knows how much you were, and continue to be, loved by all who knew you, but especially by me and your three beautiful children: Henry, Christopher and Samantha. Our children are an inspiration.

Henry (18) and Christopher (about to be 17) have just returned from eight nights sailing on a boat completely open to the elements, part of an Outward Bound course arranged by Tuesday's Children. You would be so proud of them. They had the most basic of supplies and thrived in frigid circumstances. The Florida Keys just had their coldest weather in 33 years! Christopher was apparently the key navigator and Henry rowed like a professional and all I could think of was the stories of your rowing days at Oxford, and the medals you won as a cox. Obviously they get that gene pool from you! Samantha (13 going on 30) of course, is not to be left out, she with the blue eyes and blond hair, takes a lot of pride in knowing she completely resembles you, though she's not too thrilled with the nose! She is a star tennis player and goalie for lacrosse and certainly has your fierce competitive streak. She and Henry seem to have the same relationship you and your sister Anne Marie had; they will kill each other over a board game, yet kill FOR each other if anyone hurts the other. And Christopher, much like I've heard about your sister Ruth, more or less laughs at them.

At dinner, we all continue to remember stories, like the time the boys were young and you found they had "borrowed" an axe from a neighbor and kept it hidden in a tree, and you made them return it and apologize. I have more or less given up on trying to make pancakes, as they only tell me that mine are not as good as the ones you made every Sunday morning with Samantha. Apparently, the two of you were like a pancake factory!

These ten years we have had much support from old friends, and made many new ones, including others who lost a loved one on 9/11. We continue to see everyone in England, Granny comes and stays regularly for a month at a time. Henry will actually be working in London this summer for five weeks as part of an internship with Villanova. Christopher and Samantha want to go work in your sister Anne Marie's pub!!

I am sure you are looking down on them with pride. They meet challenges head on, thrive despite obstacles placed in front of them, and never forget that the choices they make each and every day are a reflection of their love for you. Their future is bright, your spirit is inside all of us. We're beating deadlines every day.

With all my love always and forever, Laura

DAVID GARCIA

David Garcia was born on May 11, 1961 in Poughkeepsie, NY, to Stanley and Hiro Garcia, the brother of Richard. He married Deborah Rieb in 1987 and they have two sons, Davin and Dylan. David earned a B.S. degree in Math and Computer Science from SUNY College at Cortland, where he met Deborah, and was working full-time as a Computer Programmer Analyst and Private Contractor for Marsh & McLennan and part-time for GHI. He was passionate about his wife, children, extended family and friends, boating, skiing and music. He also had strong interests in self-improvement, securing a financial future for his family and finding a cure for Retinits Pigmentosa and the Foundation Fighting Blindness. On September 11, 2001, David was on his way to his desk on the 97th Floor of Tower 1. He was 40 years of age.

Davin Garcia (son)
Age: 18

Dear Dad,

Each 9/11 anniversary when I think of the day of September 11th 2001, the most vivid of memories re-appear in my mind like they were planted there yesterday. Only it they weren't planted there yesterday, but a full nine years ago. Although most of the most momentous and memorable times have passed in my personal life, when I am re-united with the same people, the same faces year after year, I can't help but think, "Where has the time gone?"

It feels like just yesterday that I was on the school bus heading to Lawrence Woodmere Academy on the morning of September 11th. You and Mom had proudly enrolled me Lawrence Woodmere Academy, a private institution just a year before. It feels like just yesterday that I was sitting in my first class of the day with my hands folded ready to absorb new information when the elementary principal entered the room. I don't remember most of the words she said but it was the quickly sketched diagram of two towers, two airplanes and two arrows on the chalk board that was burned in my mind. It was just yesterday I was riding on the bus back home and listening to my peers saying "everything will be fine, I promise!"

The time of my life leading up to the attacks and the time after are separated like intervals in my mind. It is like I lived another lifetime before and after I was born once again into a similar life only with a piece missing. The memories we shared and the daily routines we continued as a complete family in the lifetime before were suddenly curtailed. Although these routines such as eating meals together and traveling together were reinstated after a while, they were never the same. For example, in 1999 we spent our first week at Bear Springs Camps in Maine. Since then, we've been making an annual pilgrimage back to the same camp in the same spot in Maine and it is hands down our favorite place to be as a family together for a whole week without TV! After you died, the trip to Maine was nearly ended but I insisted we go even though we lost much and the trip would never be the same. I will never forget fishing trips on the small aluminum boats pulling fish in so fast there was no time to release them. Each trip to Maine is especially reminiscent because of the memories I so colorfully remember.

Even though you suffered from legal blindness, you never let anyone take advantage of you. You were a man who got what he wanted and always looked to the positive. You never let anyone stand in the way of your dream whether it was owning a boat or coaching a little league baseball team. You were strong and able bodied and I could count on you to do anything whether it was teach me to pitch or have a Lego war. I've learned to never let anyone tell me what I can't do and pursue any passion I dream of.

I hope to carry on your legacy which is to be a well-rounded and independent individual. I want to contribute and help people like you would, donating to charities and helping a neighbor fix a car. Dad, although your departure was much too soon, I thank you for the invaluable impact you made on me and my outlook on life. Although I had only known you for so little, you have shaped me as a human being unlike anyone else on the planet and that's how incredible you were.

Thank you again and I love you Dad, always and forever.

JEFFREY P. WALZ

Jeffrey P. Walz was born on March 29th, 1964 in Staten Island, New York to Raymond and Jennie Walz, the brother of Raymond and Karen. His first day on the New York City Fire Department was January 1, 1993 assigned to Ladder 9; the house he both started and ended his career in. He and his wife Rani married in October of 1995, and welcomed their son, Bradley in May of 1998. Jeffrey loved his family, working part-time as an electrical engineer working on aircraft carrier catapult systems for the US Navy in Lakehurst, New Jersey, the New York Giants and being a member of the FDNY. Jeff was posthumously promoted to Lieutenant shortly after 9/11 . . . he never had the honor of wearing the white lieutenant's hat. He was in Tower 2 and was 37 years old

Rani Walz (Wife)

Dear Jeff,

I can't believe almost ten years have passed since you were taken away from your family and friends, not to mention the life you had to live. Time has gone rapidly, and yet in so many ways, stands motionless. I can still see your face, hear your voice and call to mind things you would say to me and, if I try really hard, I can actually hear you saying them. It is soothing and brings some reassurance that you are close by.

There is so much to write and not enough time and or space, so I will try to be as brief as I can. Ten years has been like a rollercoaster ride—ups, downs, twists and many drops! The coaster does stop and we get off and from time to time but then the ride begins again! Although you know how much I love those rides, this one isn't holding the thrill that the amusement parks have. To this day, I am "SO" not amused.

This year has so much in store for us and especially for Bradley, preparing and studying for his Bar Mitzvah. I know this will be a hard day for all—feeling your absence. With each and every milestone Bradley faces, I am saddened that you are not here to witness and be part of it, not just for you, but for Bradley. In my heart, I know you and your son would have been buddies! He is a sports guru and I totally would not have existed during football season! And, guess what? That would have been so heartwarming to see you both chilling on the couches in the football trance and discussing plays, let alone yelling at the television. If only.

Life has had many ups and downs and I have made a nice life for Bradley and myself. I "know" this is what you would have wanted and "expect no less".

Let me begin with our precious baby Bradley. Not a baby anymore! Bradley has turned into a wonderful young man at the age of 12. "Brad" as he likes to be called, (and yes, I swore up and down that I would never allow that) has, in a short 12 years, conquered so many obstacles and struggles dealing with your passing, not to mention the struggles of just growing up. He has the same passion for baseball that you had for mountain biking. How proud you would be sitting at the games watching and observing. I often sit and watch him and smile to myself and visualize the smile you would have on your face; and then I get so sad by your absence, I look up to the sky and somehow "know "you are looking down.

Bradley does well in school and puts his best foot forward. He often asks me if I think "Daddy would be proud?"

"How could he not," is my response. "You are an amazing child through and through and when the stars are glistening, that is your Dad's smile."

Jeff, it is time to wrap up this letter, and so, for me—well, I am still trying to figure out a life for myself, and in time I will. I have focused so much time on our Bradley that although I had an opportunity for me, it wasn't the right time and place. One day, my turn will come or at least I hope so and in my heart I know or I hope you would want that for me and approve. In the past I have struggled with that, but that has changed. You will "always" have a part of my heart forever and I will always "love you" and "keep you close".

I love you—Rani A/K/A Pooh